Amateur
Furniture Construction

Also by the Author

The Repair and Reupholstering of Old Furniture

Amateur
Furniture Construction

by Vernon M. Albers

South Brunswick and New York: A. S. Barnes and Co.
London: Thomas Yoseloff Ltd

A.S. Barnes and Co., Inc.
Cranbury, New Jersey 08512

Thomas Yoseloff Ltd
108 New Bond Street
London W1Y OQX, England

First Printing February, 1970
Second Printing October, 1970

ISBN: 0-498-07389-0
Printed in the United States of America

Contents

Preface

There is a growing interest in hobbies in America because of the increase in the amount of leisure time available to large numbers of people. Many people, in their quests for hobbies, are interested in doing something constructive. This accounts for the increased interest in woodcraftsmanship.

Woodcraftsmanship is a hobby which can be engaged in with either a simple and inexpensive outlay of tools and equipment or an elaborate assemblage of power tools. Early professional craftsmen worked entirely with hand tools, and the still-extant results of their work bear witness to the fact that power tools are not essential to the attainment of fine craftsmanship. Power tools, however, permit you to obtain the same results with much less expenditure of time and labor. The hobbyist planning to engage in woodworking should purchase his tools with care, always remembering that a power tool requires adequate space if it is to provide its potential contribution.

Woodworking has an appeal to many people because beautiful things can be fabricated from wood. Wood is a material which continually challenges the skill of a craftsman because no two pieces of it behave in the same way.

The beginning woodcraftsman should start with the construction of simple things and gradually progress to the more complicated. As his skill increases, his interest in his hobby will increase. Regardless of the degree of skill he has attained, the amateur furniture builder will continually encounter new problems to be solved.

It is possible to build furniture from available designs, but the creative amateur will eventually wish to create designs of his own so that his hobby can become an art as well as a craft.

I became interested in the building of furniture when I took a course in manual arts in high school nearly fifty years ago. I have constructed many pieces of furniture, several of which required approximately two years to complete. I never go to my shop to work on a project unless I want to. If a man goes to work on a project because he feels it is his duty, the project becomes a job rather than a hobby.

Amateur
Furniture Construction

1
Introduction

1.1 AMATEUR FURNITURE-BUILDING

This book is written for amateurs. Its purpose is to acquaint the amateur with the proper tools and procedures for their use in fabricating furniture and cabinets of wood. Furniture and cabinetwork may be done with either hand tools or power tools. In general, the fundamental methods of woodworking and wood joining are the same whether hand tools or power tools are used except in factories where methods are applied to produce large numbers of the same item. The most important difference between hand tool-work and power tool-work is the amount of physical labor and time involved. It may appear that less skill is necessary when power tools are used. In practice there is little difference in the levels of skill required except, often, in the way in which the skills are applied.

It is possible to do fine work with hand tools. An amateur who is not in a position to use power tools should not feel that he is therefore denied the opportunity of enjoying the pleasures of woodworking.

You may be interested in building reproductions of antique furniture or some simple items needed in your home. Although the finished products may differ greatly in appearance, the fundamentals of wood joining and woodworking will be similar in your fabrication of each.

If you are interested in antiques, a book entitled *Fur-*

niture Antiques Found In Virginia by Ernest C. Lynch, Jr. (Milwaukee: The Bruce Publishing Co., 1954) is a good source of designs, with working drawings of a number of museum pieces. In many instances, you will see a piece of furniture appealing to you which you will wish to modify in design in order to meet your requirements.

Woodworking is a craft which becomes more interesting as you pursue it. Unlike homogeneous materials such as metals and plastics, no two pieces of wood are alike. The physical properties of wood are different in different directions. You will soon learn that it is important to select pieces of wood so that their different grain patterns, inclusions, and even knots fall in areas where they can be most effective in enhancing the appearance of a finished piece. In doing this your skill will improve. It requires experience to visualize the appearance of a final surface.

1.2. WOOD

Wood of local varieties is available as lumber in rough form from small sawmills. There are dealers who can supply very fine grades of lumber for furniture making and there are others who can supply plywoods in various hardwoods.

The hardwoods—which are products of deciduous trees such as maple, oak, walnut, cherry and mahagony—are those most commonly used in furniture making. The softwoods from evergreen trees—pine, fir, and redwood—are used in some furniture and also to a large extent in cabinet making. Plywood is manufactured by gluing together alternate layers of woods whose grains run perpendicular to each other. Plywood, in thicknesses from ⅛″ to ¾″, is most commonly used. Plywood may be three-ply, five-ply, or seven-ply. It may be obtained in finish quality on both sides or only one side. Hardwoods may be obtained as special plywood, with a layer of the finish wood on each side and solid lumber in between, plus thin layers of wood with right-angled grains on either side of the center.

The material for plywood is cut by shaving a layer from around and around a log while the wood is still green. Its grain-pattern is different from that of a piece of lumber cut in the ordinary way from the same wood. The reader is referred to *The Craftsman In Wood* by Edward H. Pinto (London: G. Bell and Sons Limited, 1962) for a thorough description of the various woods and wood-products.

Much of the lumber used in furniture making is sawed and milled to either ¾" or 13/16" thickness. I usually work with cherry or walnut because I like them and they are native to the region where I live. I get the lumber rough-sawed from farmers or small mills. I have the boards milled to 13/16" at a local mill. In addition to these—which should have been seasoned for two or three years before they were milled—I always have some milled to ½" and others to 2" or 3" for use in making furniture legs. This thick material is left in rough-sawed condition.

Cherry lumber was frequently used in making Early American furniture. It is a very hard wood, difficult to work, and quite susceptible to warping. It is light in color when first cut but darkens with age to a beautiful reddish brown.

Walnut is not as hard as cherry. It is considerably easier to work. And it is not as subject to warping. It has a wide range of color, varying from almost black to brown and reddish brown. There is little or no change in its color with time, except that exposure to strong sunlight sometimes causes bleaching.

Maple and birch are white, hard, fine-grained woods, not very subject to warping. They are structurally strong. They are used where a strong white wood is desired or where the wood is to be painted or stained. They are relatively easy to work.

Pine has had considerable use in certain types of furniture where a soft white wood is desired. It is easy to work, but much care must be exercised to avoid denting the surface. It is widely used in cabinet work both as lumber and as plywood when the cabinets are to be painted.

Oak is a hard coarse-grained wood. It is used for certain kinds of heavy furniture and also for the hidden structure of upholstered furniture. Much English furniture was made of oak. Styles of furniture for which oak is appropriate would not look right if fabricated from mahogany or walnut.

Mahogany is not a wood native to North America. There are several kinds such as Mexican, Hondura, and Philippine, which vary in hardness and color. Mahogany is easy to work. It usually is stained red, although it is beautiful when finished in its natural color. Since it is imported, it is generally more expensive than native woods.

1.3. TOOLS

Some tools are essential to any kind of furniture-making. Some are not essential but desirable to have. Others are essential to specific operations which you may or may not wish to do.

Even though you may wish to invest in power tools, before you start to do anything you will need hand tools.

Acquire them first. They are listed in Table 1.

Table I
Hand Tools Necessary for Any Woodworking

1 small hammer
1 wood or plastic mallet
4 chisels—¼″, ½″, ¾″, and 1″
1 six- or eight-foot steel tape
1 6″ steel scale with one scale divided in 1/32″
1 8″ try square
1 12″ combination square
1 marking gauge
1 pencil compass
1 brace and 3 wood bits—¼″, ⅜″ and ½″
1 small back saw or miter saw with 11 points or more per inch
1 8 point-per-inch hand saw
1 coping saw
1 center punch
1 6″ silicon-carbide sharpening-stone—fine on one side and coarse on the other

The list of tools in Table 1 will cost about forty-five dollars. Tools of good quality should be purchased, since it is bad economy to purchase poor tools. There are other items you will need eventually, but it is best to purchase them as they are needed. For example, you can purchase other sizes of wood bits individually as you need them; you may need to add a 14″ plane and a block plane if you do not have a power jointer; you will need clamps when you are ready to glue your woodwork together, but they should be purchased in the necessary sizes as they are needed.

If you plan to purchase power tools, you should consider what the various power tools can do for you, the space required for them, and what they will cost. A list of power tools available to the amateur is given in Table 2.

Table II
Power Tools Available to the Amateur

1 bench saw
1 radial arm saw
1 jointer
1 hand power saw
1 band saw
1 lathe
1 drill press
1 power-belt sander
1 router
1 shaper
1 hand electric drill
1 saber saw
1 shop vacuum cleaner
1 work bench

Before you go out and purchase all of the tools listed in Table 2, which will cost several hundred dollars, you must consider if you will really have use for them. As we examine the various woodworking operations with hand tools and power tools, you will be able to decide which ones you will wish to purchase.

If you purchase any single power tool, it should be a saw. This may be a bench saw or a radial arm saw. I believe that, for the amateur, the bench saw is preferable. Unless you are setting up a very large shop, you should not invest in both types. A bench saw, in addition to providing a precise means of cutting lumber, can be used with several accessories to do operations such as molding-cutting, tenon-cutting, dado-cutting, and sharpening of saw and jointer blades.

The common sizes of bench saws are 8″ and 10″. The size refers to the maximum diameter of saw which can be used. The 10″ saw, however, has a larger table area and is therefore superior to the 8″ saw in more respects than the depth of cut which it can make. Some bench saws are made with a tilting table. Others have a permanently horizontal table with provision for tilting the arbor which holds the saw. I have used both types and prefer the tilting-arbor saw because it is easier than handling large pieces of lumber on a tilted table.

A jointer may be purchased as a separate item or as an attachment to a saw with the same motor used to operate both tools. The smallest you should consider is 4" wide, with a tilting fence.

A hand power-saw is useful in cabinetwork if you need to cut up a large number of sheets of plywood. It is very difficult to handle a 4' x 8' sheet of plywood on a bench saw, but if you need to handle such material only occasionally the cutting can be done effectively with the hand saw.

A band saw can be used to cut curves and for rapid cut-off of small pieces where high precision is not required. The band saw can be used with several types of blades; including metal-cutting blades. If metal cutting is to be done, you must have a speed reducer on the motor because metal-cutting blades must be operated at about one-tenth of the speed of wood-cutting blades.

If you plan to do any wood turning, a lathe will be necessary. Wood-turning lathes are much cheaper than metal-turning lathes. They are better suited to wood turning than are metal-turning lathes because they can be operated at higher speeds.

A drill press is an important tool in the shop. Besides providing a means of drilling holes accurately, the drill press can—with special attachments—do most of the operations of a shaper; with a mortising attachment, it can be used to make the rectangular holes necessary for mortise and tenon joints. To be most useful the drill press should be 14" or more. If it is to be used as a shaper, it should be very rugged.

A power-belt sander is nice to have because it can save considerable physical labor. If the dust generated by the sander is bothersome, it can be greatly minimized if the sander is equipped with a vacuum dust-pickup. Great care must be exercised in the use of a power-belt sander because it removes wood so fast that you can easily dig furrows in your work. Although sanding by hand is slower and more laborious, it is much easier to control.

A router is a specialized tool which usually is not sufficiently useful in an amateur's shop to justify its purchase. This is also true of the shaper.

A hand electric drill, in either the ¼" or ⅜" size, is very useful, however. Since the ⅜" drill is little more expensive than the ¼" drill, the additional power available is well worth the difference in cost. It is possible to purchase a saw attachment for cutting plywood sheets, a speed reducer for use with large drills, and a saber saw attachment which can do many of the operations normally done with a band saw.

Although a saber saw can be purchased as a separate tool, the needs of the amateur can be adequately met by a saber saw attachment for the small hand electric drill.

While a vacuum cleaner is not a necessity, it is a great convenience in keeping the shop clean.

A workbench is not, properly speaking, a tool, but it is an essential part of a woodworking shop. It is possible to purchase a bench ready for assembly. But I prefer—because of the added rigidity—a bench mounted on cement block piers. Its top should be made of fir structural lumber planks 2" thick. The working surface will be much improved if the top is covered with oak flooring. If the bench is built on concrete block piers, 8" x 8" x 16" blocks can be used to build a pier 32″ front-to-back and 32″ high. The bench can be built long enough so that a turning lathe can be mounted on one end and the other a woodworking vise where hand work can be done.

1.4. SAFETY

It is important to develop good safety habits early. Because of the physical properties of wood and the high speeds of most power tools, woodworking can be hazardous if proper precautions are not observed.

Never try to push a chisel through wood toward your hand. Never wear a necktie in a shop. It is a good idea to wear short-sleeved shirts when working with power tools. Women should always wear caps which completely contain the hair, especially when they are using a drill press or lathe. When using a bench saw, always hold the work firmly down on the table and do not reach over to the back of the saw while it is running. To prevent injury from a kickback, stand a little to one side of the line of the saw when cutting. If your children or your friends are watching you, never allow them to stand back of you in line with the saw. You should have safety glasses to wear when sawing or wood turning.

The most important safeguard is the development of good safety habits. Always think through a job to be certain that you are not endangering yourself or an onlooker. With experience you will find that safe methods will become second nature. Remember that if you are driving a saw with a one-horsepower motor and you pinch a piece of wood on the saw, the saw will throw it at you with enough violence to do a great deal of bodily harm. Never try to cut a piece of wood on a bench saw without using either the rip fence or the miter to control it.

Never allow children to use either hand or power tools without adequate supervision. Woodworking tools are not toys. They are potentially dangerous implements and should always be treated as such.

Manuals are always supplied with power tools. These manuals explain the capabilities of the tools, how to keep them in proper adjustment, how to operate them safely. Whenever there is a question in your mind about the proper method of operating a tool, consult the manual.

It is important for all electric wiring in a shop equipped with power tools to be three-wire—that is, it should have two power leads and a ground lead. Receptacles should all accept three-prong plugs. All plugs connecting tools to receptacles should be three-wire. Power cords for the tools should be three-wire, with the ground wire connected to the motor frame. If your present receptacles will accept only two-prong plugs, you should have your electrician find out if a ground wire is wired into the receptacle boxes. If it is, wiring in three-wire receptacles is a simple matter. If there is no ground wire, the electrician can easily run one to all of your receptacle boxes and ground it through a water pipe.

This precaution is important because all tools are made of metal, and if one of the terminals in a motor shorts to the frame it can result in serious injury or even death to the operator when the frame is not properly grounded. Any extension cord should be three-wire, since extension cords often need to be used with hand electric drills, which are particularly dangerous.

2

Principles of Mechanical Design

2.1 INTRODUCTION

When an engineer designs a bridge, he is supplied with accurate information about the stresses to which it will be subjected by the loads it is expected to carry, by winds, by potential earthquakes. Furniture, on the other hand, is subjected to many severe stresses which cannot be predicted. The bridge-designing engineer is permitted to use diagonal members in his structure, but there are very few instances in which the furniture builder can use them; such members interfere with functional use of the furniture or are unacceptable because of appearance. Furniture designs have evolved over hundreds of years, and the success of furniture designers in solving the difficult problem of producing furniture which is functional and of adequate strength as well as pleasing in appearance has been proved by the many pieces we have which have been in service for more than 100 years.

For a piece of furniture to be acceptable, it must perform a useful function and be artistically attractive in its surroundings.

Nearly all wood in furniture is joined with glue. There are a few instances in which screws must be used; these will be discussed in future chapters. The strength of a glued joint is dependent on the properties of the glue, the accuracy of fit of the joint, and the nature of the stresses applied to the joint. A piece of dried glue by itself is not very strong, but when two surfaces of wood make contact with each other by means of a film of glue, the junction is stronger than the surrounding wood. Because of this, the importance of accuracy in the fit of joints to be glued cannot be overemphasized.

2.2. THE THREE KINDS OF STRESSES

We can divide the stresses to which a joint can be subjected into three kinds. They are: shear, tension, and compression. There will normally be some combination of these in any particular application.

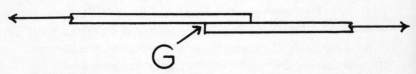

Fig. 2.1. A shear stress on a glued joint. The pieces are glued together at G, and the external forces are exerted in the direction of the arrows.

Figure 2.1 shows an example of a shear stress on a glued joint. A well-prepared glued joint will withstand very high shear stresses. Several of the standard glued joints are designed to have fairly large areas subject to shear stress in the normal use of the furniture.

Figure 2.2 shows an example of a tension stress on a glued joint. Although the glued joint may be stronger than the adjoining woods, such a joint will fail due to separation of the wood fibres under tension stress. We avoid, insofar as possible, designs which have a great

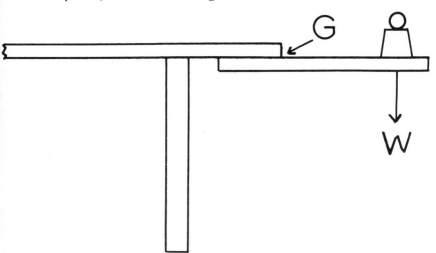

Fig. 2.2. A tension stress on a glued joint. The pieces are glued together at G, and the stress is exerted by the weight in the direction of the arrow.

dependence on the tension strength of glued joints.

Figure 2.3 shows an example of a compression stress on a glued joint. If the joint is properly made, such a stress will not cause the joint to fail until the strength of the wood is exceeded. Since the compressive strength of the joint far exceeds that of the wood, joints should be designed so that compressive stresses are involved.

We will discuss in the next chapter the various types of standard glued joints used in furniture. We will see that these joints have been evolved to make the maximum use of the desirable characteristics of shear and compressive stresses.

The strength of a wooden member in a piece of furniture will depend on the direction of stresses in relation to the direction of the grain in the wood. For example, a

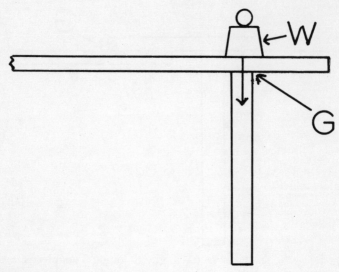

Fig. 2.3. A compression stress on a glued joint. The pieces are glued together at G, and the load is applied in the direction of the arrow.

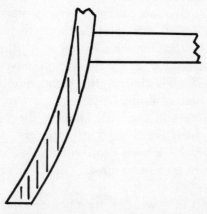

Fig. 2.4. Curved chair leg showing how the grain of the wood may run in relation to the configuration of the leg. The lines indicate the direction of the grain.

chair leg, which is vertical and cut so that the grain of the wood is parallel to the axis of the leg, can support a very heavy load. However, if the leg is shaped like that shown in Fig. 2.4, with the grain running in the direction indicated, the strength of the leg will be much reduced because the wood will tend to separate parallel to the grain under shear and tension stresses caused by a lighter load. Many chairs are designed in the manner of the one shown in Fig. 2.4. When this has to be done, the wood must be selected with great care so that pieces weakened by knots in the area of the cross grain are not used.

2.3. MOMENTS OF FORCES

When a piece of furniture is in use, the forces to which

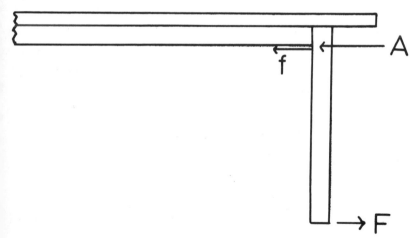

Fig. 2.5. Moments of forces on a table leg. If the leg is 32″ long and the width of the stringers between the legs is 2″, f × 2 = F × 32 or f = F × 32/2.

some portions of its structure are subjected may be much greater than those applied to other of its parts. For example, consider the table leg shown in Fig. 2.5. If the table is dragged across the floor, a force F will be exerted in the direction of the arrow by the reaction between the leg and the floor. In order to counteract this force, a force f must be exerted at A. If point A is 2″ below the top of the table and the leg is 32″ long, the force f will be sixteen times as great as F. It is important that the forces to which the piece of furniture is subjected are not applied to such long-moment arms that excessive forces will result at some point in its structure.

2.4. BEAMS

Acted on by a force F, a beam like the one shown in Fig. 2.6 will have the following stiffness:

$$S = bd^3/l^3.$$

If we consider a beam between two legs of a table and assume that it is a piece of lumber ¾″ thick, 4″ wide and 48″ long, with b ¾″ and d 4″, its stiffness will be 1/2304. If we turn the beam so that b is 4″ and d is ¾″, its stiffness will be 1/65536. The beam will therefore be about twenty-four times as stiff—as a load-bearing element—if the wide dimension is vertical. This is one reason why stringers are installed between legs on tables and chairs with the wide dimension vertical. A second reason is that this wider dimension provides the greatest moment of force to compensate for forces developed at the bottom ends of the legs. If the furniture is to be subjected to hard use, stringers between the legs near the bottom will greatly increase the strength of the structure. You will find there are some chairs with lower stringers and

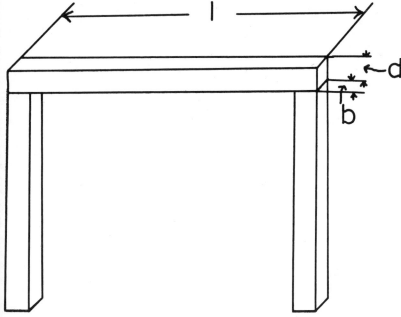

Fig. 2.6. A beam supported at its ends.

some without. Generally, those designed without lower stringers are intended for much less rough usage.

3

Joints

3.1. INTRODUCTION

If you examine a variety of pieces of furniture, you will find that all of them have been constructed by means of a limited number of kinds of components and that all these components have been put together by certain standard glued joints. In this chapter, I will describe the construction of the six kinds of glued joints used in furniture. I recommend that before building a piece of furniture you make samples of any joints you intend to use in it.

3.2. THE SIX STANDARD GLUED JOINTS

3.2.1. THE CROSS LAPPED JOINT

The cross lapped joint is the simplest to make, but it does not have many uses. To make a sample, select two pieces of lumber about 6″ long, 2″ wide, and ¾″ thick. You are going to join them by cutting out both pieces as shown in Fig. 3.1. The depth of the cutouts are first marked with the marking gauge set at ⅜″. Mark both pieces from the top with the same setting of the gauge to insure that when the pieces are fitted together the surfaces at the top will be in exactly the same plane.

If the joint is to be made with hand tools, after the depth of the cutout has been marked with the marking gauge, mark the edges of the cutout with a try square

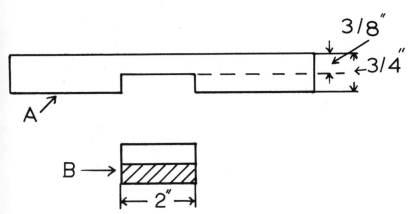

Fig. 3.1. Formation of a cross lapped joint.

and a sharp pencil so that the distance between the marks is equal to the width of the piece which will fit into the cutout. A cut should now be made with a small back saw down to the marks made with the marking gauge. Remember that a saw cuts a slot of finite width. Therefore saw so that the outside edges of the cut are on the lines marking its width. In this way the width of the cutout will be exactly equal to the width of the piece which is to fit into it. The two pieces will now appear as shown in Fig. 3.2. Now clamp each piece firmly in a vise and with a 1″ chisel and a mallet, cut out the portion between the saw

Fig. 3.2. Saw cuts for a cross lapped joint.

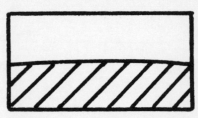

Fig. 3.3.. Rounded section through a cross lapped joint which should be avoided.

cuts. Do not try to cut out the full depth all at once because this may cause the grain of the wood to split the piece. It is important that the surface at the bottom of the cutout be exactly at the mark made by the marking gauge and that it be flat. There is a tendency for the amateur to leave the surface rounded, as in the cross section shown in Fig. 3.3. This can be checked with a try square. If the joint is properly prepared, there will be a large area of contact to be glued.

I have used this type of joint in two instances. The first was a small child's table which was constructed of redwood and painted. The construction details are shown in Fig. 3.4. The crosshatched area in Fig. 3.4 A is the

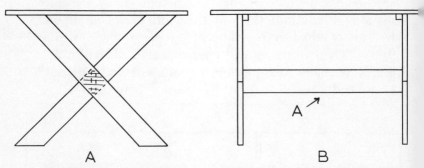

A   B

Fig. 3.4. An application of the cross lapped joint in the construction of a child's table.

area of the cross lapped joint. Fig. 3.4B is the other view of the table, showing the stringer A, which adds stiffness to the structure. The stringer A was attached to the legs at the midpoint of the cross lapped joints with mortise and tenon joints, which will be described in the next section.

The second instance in which I have used a cross lapped joint was in the construction of the base of the music stand shown in Fig. 3.5. The base was made of two pieces about 18″ long, 2″ wide, and ¾″ thick. The upright post was cut from a piece 1¾″ square, and ¾″ inch of the lower end was turned down to 1″ diameter in a lathe. A hole 1″ in diameter was bored through the center of the cross lapped joint after it was glued, and the turned end of the post was glued in place. The turned end of the post serves as a reinforcement for the cross lapped joint.

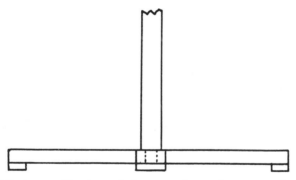

Fig. 3.5. An application of the cross lapped joint in the construction of the base for a music stand.

The cutouts for cross lapped joints can be made on a power saw. Adjust the depth of the saw cut carefully, using a piece of scrap lumber to test it. Then make the

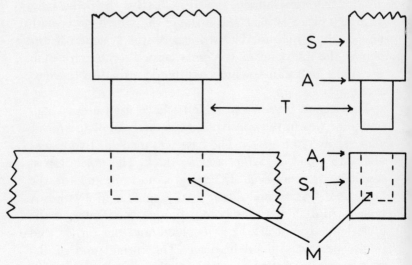

Fig. 3.6. Detail of a mortise and tenon joint.

cutout, holding the piece upon the miter on the saw and cutting successively until you have obtained the exact width of the cutout. With some types of saw blades, it will be necessary to smooth off the bottom of the cutout with a chisel.

3.2.2. MORTISE AND TENON JOINTS

The mortise and tenon joint shown in Fig. 3.6 is the most common joint used in furniture. It is difficult to find a piece of furniture which does not contain some mortise and tenon joints. This is a very strong joint if accurately made because the tenon fits the mortise so that the forces exerted on the glued joint are almost purely shear.

The thickness of the tenon is generally made about half the thickness of the lumber. If ¾″ or 13/16″ lumber is used,

the tenon can be made ⅜″ thick. If surfaces S and S_1 in
Fig. 3.6 are to be flush, shoulders A and A_1 must be made
of exactly the same width to minimize the amount of
sanding to be done later. There are, however, many instances where shoulder A_1 is about ⅛″ wider than shoulder
A. If it is possible to design the joint in this way, by all
means do so.

To construct the joint, the mortise hole should be made
first. Mark the long edges of the hole with the marking
gauge. Mark the ends by means of a try square and a
sharp pencil. If the mortise is to be made with hand tools,
its center line should also be marked with the marking
gauge. A row of holes should now be bored. Use a wood
bit of diameter equal to the width of the mortise. The centers of these holes can be close enough so that there is a
slight overlap, as shown in Fig. 3.7. If you try to overlap
them too much, however, the bit will slide over into the
adjoining hole instead of boring straight down. Do not
try to drill these holes with a twist drill because it is not
possible to keep such a drill accurately centered even
with a drill press. The old-fashioned brace and bit is the
most accurate tool for boring a hole because it has a
screw center which guides the bit and keeps it centered.
You can mark the bit for the proper depth with a piece
of adhesive or masking tape. You should clamp the work

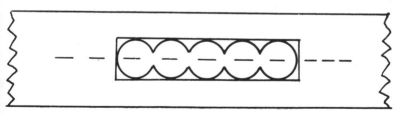

Fig. 3.7. Detail of holes to be bored in making a mortise.

firmly in a vise, keeping the surface in which the mortise is to be made accurately horizontal. This can be checked with the level in your combination square. It is important to keep the bit vertical while boring the holes. This also can be checked by sighting across the bit toward a corner or door or window in two approximately perpendicular directions.

After the holes have been bored, use the ¼" or 1" chisel and the mallet to remove wood left at the ends and between the holes. Always drive the chisel vertically downward, with its flat side toward the side of the mortise. Do not prize the chisel against the top edge of the mortise because this will deform the wood. Always prize the chisel toward the center of the mortise. Always be certain that the chisel is sharp.

The end of the piece on which the tenon is to be cut is marked with the marking gauge, as shown in Fig. 3.8.

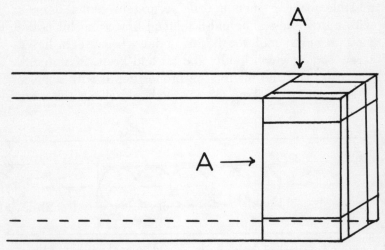

Fig. 3.8. Detail of wood to be removed to make a tenon.

Mark the lines A, using the try square and a sharp pencil. Saw along the lines A with the back saw so that the edge of the cut is on the lines. Saw down to the marks made with the marking gauge on all four sides. Remove the excess wood with the 1″ chisel, following the same procedure used in removing excess wood in the cross lapped joint. Remove the wood in thin layers, keeping the surfaces flat. When you are close to the marks, test the fit of the tenon in the mortise. The tenon should fit snugly but not so tightly that it has to be driven in. Be certain that the tenon does not hit bottom in the mortise before its shoulders make contact with the wood surface around the mortise. The joint should usually be designed so that the tenon is about 1″ long and the mortise about 1/16″ deeper.

It is possible to make mortise and tenon joints with power tools. If you have a drill press, you can purchase a mortising attachment which has various sizes of mortising bits. When purchasing a drill press, it is a good idea to check with the dealer to be certain that a mortising attachment can be obtained for the model you are considering. The mortising tool does not need to be bought at the same time as the drill press, but if a tool cannot be obtained to fit the press you may be disappointed later. The mortising tool consists of a hollow square chisel with a bit revolving in the center. The chisel cuts a square hole. The bit carries the wood up and discharges it through a hole in the side of the chisel. The mortise is made by cutting a series of square holes which start at one end of the mortise and end at the other. It is possible to cut very accurate mortises with such a tool. If you purchase one, detailed instructions for its use are furnished with it.

The tenon can be cut on a power saw in the same way as the cutout for the cross lapped joint. Or you can buy a tenon jig for use on the saw. The tenon jig is a very fine tool which can be used to cut tenons very precisely, but it requires a considerable amount of skill and setup time. If I am making a single mortise and tenon joint, I can make the tenon with hand tools in the time it takes to set up the saw and tenon jig properly. However, if you are constructing a complicated piece of furniture involving several mortise and tenon joints, a tenon jig will be worth the purchase. Detailed instructions for its use will be furnished with it.

3.2.3. DOWEL PIN JOINTS

Dowel pin joints are often used where mortise and tenon joints are. When a piece of furniture is assembled, you can not tell a mortise and tenon joint from a dowel pin joint. The choice is a matter of convenience, since the two kinds of joints have about the same strength. The dowel pin joint is perhaps easier to make, particularly if the joint is to be made with hand tools. Following are the steps necessary in making a dowel pin joint.

1. The two holes indicated by the dotted lines in part A of Fig. 3.9 are bored with care to keep the bit perpendicular to the edge of part A, following the procedure described for boring holes for a mortise.

2. A center marker like that shown in Fig. 3.10 is inserted in one of the holes. These markers can be purchased in sizes corresponding to the various sizes of wood bits. The marker of the proper size is pushed into the hole to the rim A. When parts A and B of Fig. 3.9 are pressed together in correct orientation, the center of one of the holes to be bored in part B will be marked by point B (Fig. 3.10) on the marker.

3. Using a wood bit and being careful to keep the bit perpendicular to the surface of part B in Fig 3.9, one

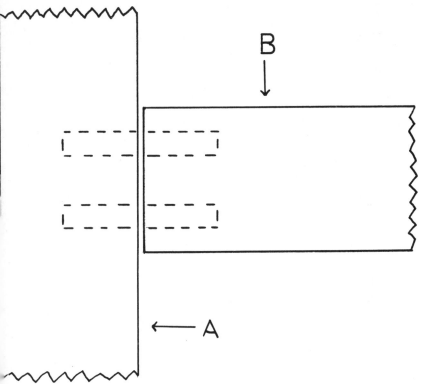

Fig. 3.9. Detail of a dowel pin joint.

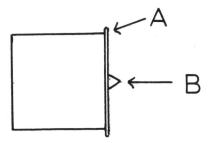

Fig. 3.10. Dowel pin center marker.

dowel pin hole is bored in part B. Remember that the axes of the dowel pin holes in the two parts must be parallel. If they are not parallel, it will be necessary for the dowel pin to bend sharply at the joint. This makes it impossible to draw the joint together without imposing severe stresses on the sides of the holes and possibly causing the wood to split.

4. Cut a dowel pin slightly shorter than the sum of the depths of the holes in parts A and B. Assemble the joint, with the dowel pin in one pair of holes in parts A and B and with the marker in the second hole of part A. This will mark the center of the second hole in part B, which can then be bored with the wood bit.

The holes should usually be from 1″ to 1¼″ deep. If the lumber thickness is ¾″, the hole should generally be ⅜″, which is one of the standard sizes of dowel pins. If the surface of contact of the joint is less than 3″ long, two dowel pins are sufficient. If it is longer, locate the dowel pin holes about 1½″ apart, with the centers of the pins at either end about ¾″ from the ends of the contact surface.

3.2.4. DOVETAIL JOINTS

The dovetail joint is a modification of the mortise and tenon joint, which does not require a long tenon to achieve great strength. It is a difficult joint to fabricate with hand tools. Its most important and almost universal application is in furniture drawers. It is also used for joining the spacers between drawers on the fronts of chests without corner posts. The reason for using dovetail joints in such instances is that, if no corner posts exist, the joint must be made directly in the side panel, which is usually only ¾″ or 13/16″ thick. The spacers between drawers must furnish a part of the rigidity of

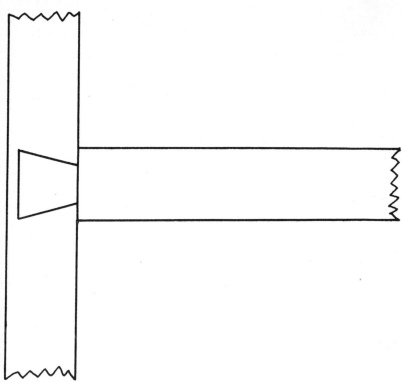

Fig. 3.11. Detail of a standard dovetail joint.

the structure in addition to support for the drawers. If mortise and tenon joints are used, it is difficult to obtain adequate strength because the mortise would be limited to a depth of about ⅜″. However, a dovetail joint of this depth will have adequate strength.

Figure 3.11 shows the form of a dovetail joint. This joint achieves its superior strength from the fact that it is a combination of shear and compression stresses. Of course, we can achieve this strength only if the fit of the joint is very precise. A mortise and tenon joint is usually made so that the tenon is completely hidden. This is not possible with a dovetail joint because its tenon must slip into the mortise from the side.

In constructing a dovetail joint with hand tools it is possible to make either the mortise or the tenon first. It is usually most convenient to make the tenon first. This is particularly true when making drawers—of which

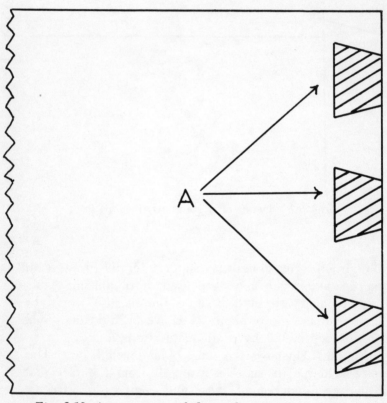

Fig. 3.12. Arrangement of dovetail joints on a drawer.

the sides, attached to both front and back, use several dovetail joints. Tenons will be cut on the ends of the side pieces. Mortises will be cut on the back and front pieces. Figure 3.12 shows the end of a side of a drawer marked for the cutting of tenons. The shaded areas are the areas to be cut out. If a drawer front is ¾" thick, the tenons are usually made ½" long so that they do not exceed it. If the sides and back of a drawer are ½" thick, the tenons will project just through the back end. The lines marking the sides of the tenons are drawn at an angle of 15° to the length of the drawer side. Cuts are made along these lines with the small back saw. The shaded areas A are then cut out with chisel and mallet. The cut should be made partly through one side and partly through the other.

After tenons have been cut on the sides of the drawer, mortises are marked on the front and back pieces. Use the tenons as patterns. Figure 3.13 shows the drawer back with the mortises marked. The wood under the shaded areas is to be removed. Removal of the wood from a mortise in a drawer front can be facilitated by boring some holes into the areas B from the back of the drawer front. Be careful not to bore too deep. Remember also that if you are using a wood bit its point projects ahead of the cutting blade: you do not want it to come through and ruin the surface. The mortise is finished with a ¼" chisel. Care and patience are needed to shape mortises so that a drawer side can slide into place with all of its tenons snugly fitting into their respective mortises. The depth—B in Fig. 3.13—should be equal the thickness of the side piece.

I have built a reproduction of a Virginia highboy which had an interesting version of the dovetail joint for joining spacers between drawers on the front. In-

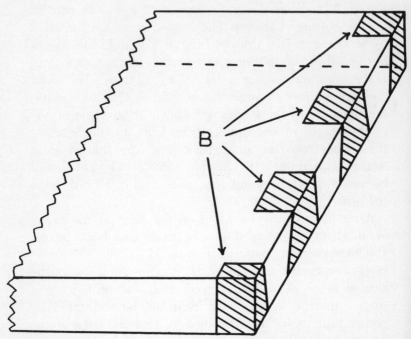

Fig. 3.13. Perspective showing cutouts marked on a drawer back.

stead of making the joints as shown in Fig. 3.11, I did as indicated in Fig. 3.14. The inset A is ⅛″ long. The dovetail tenon is ½″ long. When carefully made, this joint is even stronger than the simple dovetail joint shown in Fig. 3.11.

Some of the cutting for dovetail joints can be done with a power saw. Since the angle on dovetail tenons is usually 15°, the saw table or arbor can be set to 15°

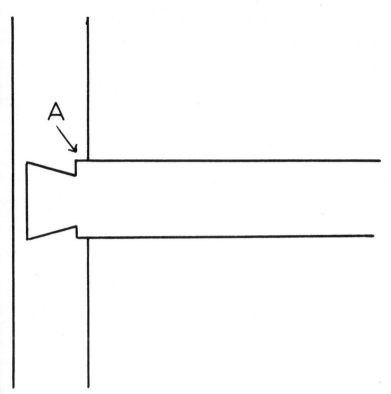

Fig. 3.14. Detail of a countersunk dovetail joint.

and the sides of the tenons cut—using a tenon jig—in the same way as described in Section 3.2.2. A router with the necessary accessories can do all of the cutting for dovetail joints, if you are prepared to spend approximately one hundred dollars for one. Unless you have a large number of such joints to make, however, I would recommend that you forego the router.

3.2.5. MITER JOINTS AND PICTURE FRAMES

Figure 3.15 shows two possible ways of joining the corners of a frame which may surround a panel, an opening, or a picture. Figure 3.15 B shows a miter joint. This joint is not as commonly used in furniture construction as one would expect. Consider the two parts a and b, which are joined by a mortise and tenon joint in the first instance and by a miter joint in the second. The grain of the wood runs lengthwise in both. As moisture content in the wood changes with the seasons, the percentage of change in the dimensions of the wood is greater across the grain than parallel with it. The corner joint in Fig. 3.15 A will fail during the first season if it is not reinforced by the tenon indicated by the dotted lines. The miter joint in Fig. 3.15 B will hold without reinforcing, however, because the line of contact, which is at an angle of 45° with the grain in both pieces, assures that the change of dimensions of both will be the same.

The most common use of miter joints is in the joining of moldings and the construction of picture frames—which, incidentally, are usually constructed of moldings. It is obvious that it is not possible to join a frame of molding by means of the joint shown in Fig. 3.15 A unless the end of part a is cut to a shape which is the inverse of the molding. This is very difficult to do.

The most difficult problem in making miter joints is accuracy. Professional cabinetmakers use a high-quality miter box equipped with a good back saw specially fitted so that it will cut a 45° angle exactly. This is expensive. For less than ten dollars it is possible to purchase a less sophisticated miter box which can be used with a back saw. It is possible to cut accurate miter joints on a power saw, of course, by use of a miter equip-

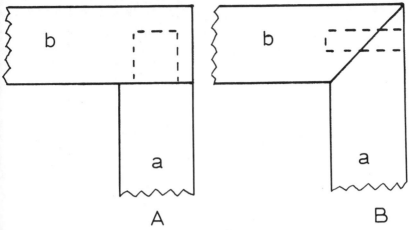

Fig. 3.15. Two methods of joining a corner.

ped with a clamp and with a tenon-cutting saw blade which is thicker and therefore more rigid than ordinary saw blades. Before cutting your pieces for the miter joint, cut a 45° angle on scrap lumber, check it with your combination square, and if necessary readjust the stops on the miter. The most crucial test for proper adjustment is to cut two pieces, one with the left miter setting and one with the right, and to check with a square to determine if together they form a 90° angle.

If you make a frame, you will have to make four miter joints. The fit of the last joint will depend on the accuracy with which you have done all your cutting.

There are some instances in which it is desirable to reinforce a miter joint. I have done this in two different ways. I usually add the reinforcement after the joint has been glued and the glue is set. In order to hold the joint while the glue sets, you can use special clamps which are available for this purpose; or you can construct a jig to hold the parts. After the glue has set, a hole can be bored from one edge with a wood bit as indicated by the dotted lines in Fig. 3.15 B. A dowel pin can then be glued in place and the end sanded flush with the wood surface. A second method of reinforcement, which can be done with a power saw, is illustrated in Fig. 3.16. A piece of scrap material A is cut to an angle of·45°. Lean the miter joint against this piece so that the bisector of the angle of the joint is perpendicular to the table. Set the fence of the saw so that the distance from the center of the blade to the fence is equal to one half the thickness of the material of the frame. Make a cut then, holding the frame rigidly against the fence and pushing the work through the saw by means of the precut piece which you use to stabilize it. Then cut a strip to the width of the saw blade (in most instances ⅛″) and glue it into the slot.

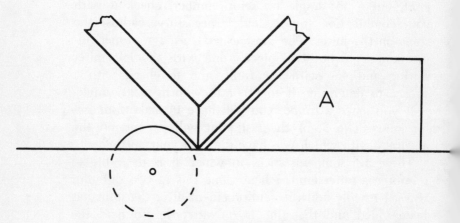

Fig. 3.16. Method of holding a corner to cut a slot with a power saw for insertion of a reinforcement.

Fig. 3.17. Form of the groove for mounting a picture in a frame or a panel in a panel frame.

You can purchase picture-frame molding which is pre-grooved for mounting both a picture and its backing. You can also make a simple frame by cutting the necessary groove with a power saw or jointer. The groove is usually ¼″ x ¼″ as illustrated in Fig. 3.17. This is also the method of forming the parts of a frame in which a panel is to be mounted.

3.2.6. PANEL AND TABLE TOP JOINTS

Unless a panel or table top is made of plywood, it will be necessary to glue a series of pieces together to obtain the width required. Lumber for such a unit is rarely completely free from warping, so your first step is to lay out the lumber so that warping in one piece will compensate for that in adjacent pieces. Figure 3.18 shows how the pieces are laid out and marked. Edges 1-2, 3-4, 5-6, etc. will be glued together. Edges 1 and 2 are first prepared with a large hand-plane or a jointer. These edges must fit together so that they make intimate contact at the

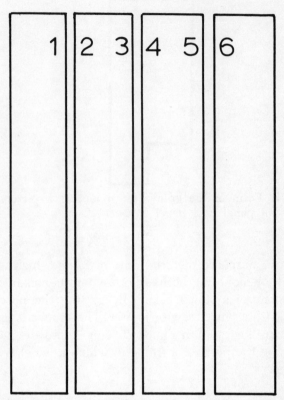

Fig. 3.18. Layout of boards prior to planing for glued joints for a table top or a panel.

ends but are slightly separated in the middle, where after being glued they will be forced together by clamps. This prevents the ends of the joints from separating during periods of low humidity. When the two pieces are put together as in Fig. 3.19, their sides must be parallel as in A they should not make an angle as in B. If both edges are precisely perpendicular, they will fit as in A. It

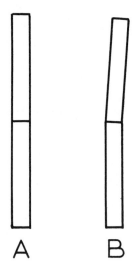

Fig. 3.19. The effect of proper and improper planing of the edges for a glued joint.

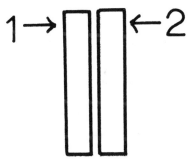

Fig. 3.20. Orientation of the two pieces for planing for a glued joint.

is, however, nearly impossible to achieve this precision. Therefore plane the two edges simultaneously, holding them as shown in Fig. 3.20. Under these conditions, if

the planed surfaces are not exactly perpendicular to the
sides the incorrect angle will be the same on both and
they will compensate for each other. With practice, it is
possible to prepare such a glued joint with a hand plane,
but it is necessary for its blade to be in excellent condition.

Surfaces can also be planed on a jointer. Again the two
pieces should be planed together as in Fig. 3.20. When
the edges for joint 1-2 have been planed, plane the edges
for joint 3-4 in the same manner, then the edges for the
joint 5-6, etc., until all of the joint surfaces have been
planed.

Glued joints are usually reinforced with dowel pins. A
minimum of three dowel pins is used in each joint. If the
joint is quite long, the pins are spaced about 10″ apart.
With the two boards clamped as in Fig. 3.20, locate the
positions of the holes for the pins and with a try square
draw a line across the edges of the boards. Now set your
marking gauge to one half the thickness of one board.
Scratch a mark on each of the lines to indicate the location of the dowel pin centers. Use the face of the marking
gauge first on the right side and then on the left side of
Fig. 3.20. With a brace and bit, bore holes at the inter-
sections of the cross marks and those of the marking
gauge. If the lumber is ¾″ thick, bore ⅜″ holes about 1½″
deep. Use ⅜″ dowel pins cut in lengths slightly less than
the sum of the depths of the two holes. If the lumber
used is less than ¾″, correspondingly smaller dowel pins
should be used. For example, use 3/16″ to ¼″ dowel pins
with ½″ lumber. When the dowel pin holes have been
bored for joint 1-2, repeat the process until all the holes
have been bored for all joints. In handling the lumber after the joints have been planed, you must be very careful
to avoid denting the surfaces.

You are now ready to try to assemble the joints. Be certain there are no wood chips in the holes. Assemble the joints with the dowel pins in place and draw them up with clamps, using three clamps, one placed near each end and one in the middle. If the joints fit correctly, you are ready to start gluing.

For glue I prefer a plastic resin powder which you mix with water when you are ready to use it. Follow the directions on the container for mixing. Be certain to mix enough glue to do the enitre job. On your first experience you will probably find you need about twice as much glue as you expect. Apply a thin layer of glue to surface 1 (Fig. 3.18), coat the dowel pins with glue, and push them into the holes. Coat surface 2 with glue, being certain that the holes are coated inside. Then push surfaces 1 and 2 together. Repeat the process until all joints have been coated and pushed together. Apply the clamps and draw the joints together as tightly as you can. In order that the unit will be flat, wood strips should be placed across its ends, with waxed paper between the strips and your assembly, and held together by two C clamps at each end. It is important to work fast so that the entire process is completed before the glue begins to set. This is why before gluing you should be certain that you have all necessary items at hand and that you will not have to stop and look for something in the midst of the process.

It is a good idea to use warm water and a rag to wash off as much of the excess glue as possible after the assembly has been clamped. This will save considerable work later. Leave the clamps on overnight.

Before attempting to assemble a unit involving many joints, practice by making a single-joint unit about two feet long. Do not be discouraged if you have trouble on your first attempt. It takes practice to develop the skill to make a good glued joint. But you should soon learn to join two pieces so well that the joint will be hardly visible after the surface is sanded flat.

When the glue has set, you will find that the surface will need to be sanded. It is impossible to locate the dowel-pin holes accurately enough for the surfaces to be exactly in a plane. Start with coarse sandpaper and finish with fine.

It is difficult to make glued joints much more than 36″ long with a hand plane or a small 4″ jointer. If you need a table top 4′ long or more, I suggest that you have it made at a professional mill where large jointers are available. When I built a pair of Sheraton banquet tables, four top sections about 2′ x 4′ were required, and I had them fabricated at a mill. They were glued and rough-sanded at the mill. I cut them to the exact size and did the fine sanding. With the facilities available at a professional mill, the cost is quite low.

3.3. SUMMARY

It will require practice to develop skill in fabricating any of the standard joints. It is best to start by building a simple piece of furniture and, as you come to each kind of joint, to use some scrap pieces of lumber and make a model of the joint and then, when you are satisfied you can make an acceptable one, go ahead. In this way you can immediately get started on something constructive. I have built furniture for many years, but I still encounter new kinds of problems—and I still make a practice model. Sometimes I have to do a lot of experimenting before I evolve a satisfactory procedure. I have always taken the attitude that I am constructing furniture for fun. I refuse to predict a completion date. If it takes me a month to work out a problem, that is part of the fun, too.

You will find at first that wood does strange things when you try to cut it with various tools. This is because no two pieces of wood have the same characteristics and even a single piece of wood has different characteristics in different directions. You need much experience to achieve high accuracy in woodworking, and the only way you can get it is by working wood. Each joint is a challenge, and I can assure you that while you may sometimes become discouraged you will never be bored.

4
Construction Units

4.1 LEGS

Nearly every piece of furniture has legs. In some instances, the legs form a part of the framework of the structure. In others, the legs serve the primary function of supporting the important part of the structure at the proper height. The legs on a chair form a part of the structure. The back of the chair is usually formed, in part, by the extension of the back legs.

Cupboards and chests have legs which are simply extensions of the corner elements of their frames. A table is the best example of furniture which has legs designed to support the functional portion of the piece at a level convenient for use. This is also true of a grand piano and of a harpsichord. If you look around at the furniture in your home, you will probably be able to cite other examples of furniture of which this is true.

4.1.1. SQUARE LEGS

The simplest kind of furniture leg is the square leg. Some square legs have the same cross-sectional dimensions at the bottom as at the top. This is true of some oak furniture. The more common form of square leg tapers so that it is more slender at the bottom than at the top. If a table is designed to have a drawer at the top as well as tapered square legs, the cross section of the leg will be uniform from the top down to the bottom of the drawer and will taper from there to the bottom of the leg.

Tapered square legs may have the same taper on all four sides. Or they may be designed so that the outside corner of a leg is vertical with its taper produced by removal of wood from only two of its sides. Figure 4.1 shows a table with tapered square legs in which the taper has been produced by removal of wood from the inner side only, leaving the two outside faces of each leg vertical.

Fig. 4.1. A small lamp-table with tapered square legs.

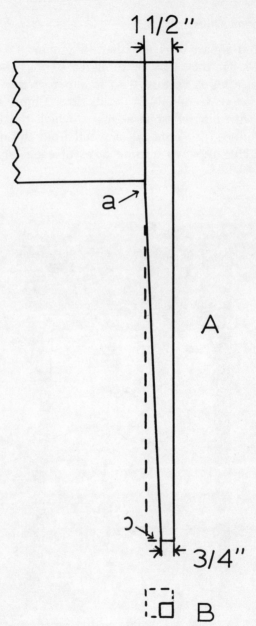

Fig. 4.2. Layout of cuts made to taper a square leg.

The legs on this table are 1½″ square from the top to the bottom of the drawer guide and from that point they taper uniformly to ¾″ squares. Figure 4.2 shows how excess wood is cut away on one side. Figure 4.2 A is a front view of the leg, Fig. 4.2 B the bottom-end view. The dotted lines show excess wood which was removed. If the leg is made with hand tools, the 1½″ square piece is marked with the line ab and the taper produced by sawing along the line ab with a hand saw, leaving a small amount of wood to be removed with a hand plane. The process is then repeated on the other inside surface.

If you have a power saw, the taper can be cut quite easily by means of a simple jig illustrated in Fig. 4.3. A is the saw fence, S is the saw blade. B is a strip of wood about 2″ x ½″ and somewhat longer than the leg. C is a piece of ¼″ material about the same width as B which is attached to the end of B with two screws. A nail D can be driven into the end of the leg to hold it in position while the cut is made. The leg and the jig are arranged on the saw table and the fence position adjusted so that when the saw cuts off the correct thickness at the bottom end of the leg the saw will run out at E, where the taper stops. Excess wood can now be cut off by pushing the jig and the leg through the saw. Turn the leg through

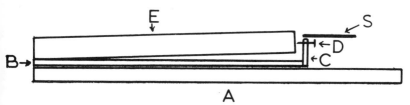

Fig. 4.3. Arrangement for cutting a taper with a table saw.

90°. With the same spacing between the jig and the bottom end of the leg, drive the nail in and saw the excess wood from the second side. The sides of the leg from which excess wood is cut are those on which mortises are cut to accept tenons to form the frame of the table.

If the legs are tapered on all four sides, the same procedure is followed, except that the depth of cut at the bottom end of the leg will be only half as great. If the leg shown in Fig. 4.2 was to be tapered on four sides, the point b would be ⅜″ from the outside. There would thus be four separate cuts made, whether by hand or with a jig on a bench saw.

If the taper is to extend all the way to the top, point a in Fig. 4.2 would be at the top end of the leg. Figure 4.4 shows a leg on a harpsichord which I constructed. This leg is tapered on all four sides, and the taper extends all the way to the top. It is 2¼″ square at the top and 1⅛″ square at the bottom.

4.1.2. TURNED LEGS

Turned legs are the most common to be found on furniture. If you will look around at the furniture in your home, you will doubtless find a variety of turned legs on chairs and tables.

It is necessary to have a lathe in order to produce turnings. It is also necessary to have adequate turning chisels. Since the piece of wood with which you start is normally square and a portion of the length is usually left square, it is important to mount the piece in the lathe so that the center points of the lathe are accurately centered in the ends of the wood. In this way the axis of the turned portion will coincide with the axis of the square portion.

You should accurately locate the centers of the lathe

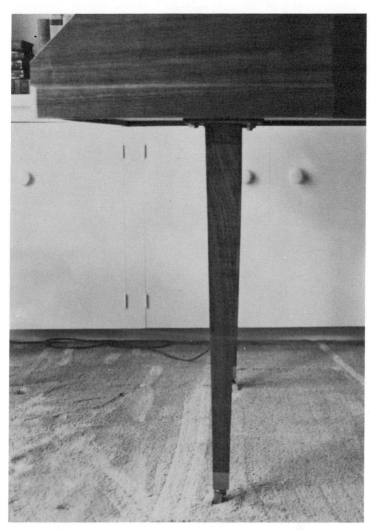

Fig. 4.4. Leg on a harpsichord. This leg is tapered on all four sides.

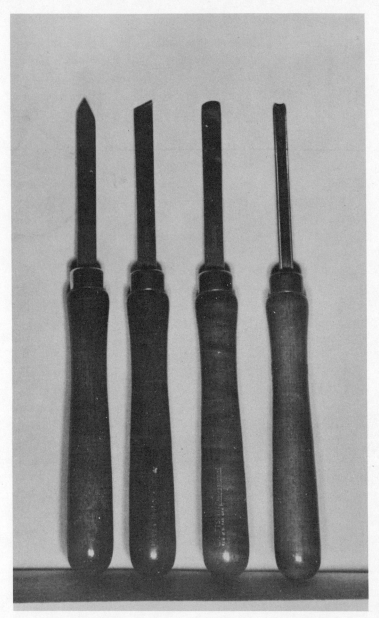

Fig. 4.5. Four shapes of standard turning chisels.

at the two ends of the piece and mark the points by means of a center punch and drill with a center bit. These can be purchased at your local hardware store. The center bit has a 60° taper which will fit the centers on the headstock and tailstock of the lathe. The wood-turning center on the headstock has claws which engage the wood so that it will turn with the headstock shaft. The tailstock center rides as a bearing in the hole at the other end of the lathe. You should apply a small amount of oil to the tailstock center so that heat will not ruin it. The center should fit into the hole tightly enough to insure that the piece of wood will not vibrate.

Figure 4.5 shows a selection of turning chisels to do various turning operations. The long heavy handles are necessary to provide leverage to hold the tool rigid on

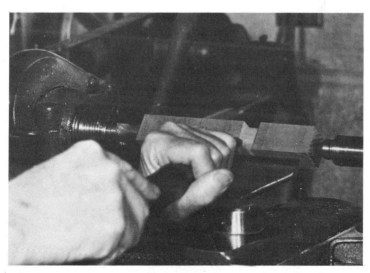

Fig. 4.6. Use of chisel #1 in Fig. 4.5 to reduce the diameter of a section.

Fig. 4.7. Use of chisel #2 in Fig. 4.5 to smooth a uniform section.

Fig. 4.8. Use of chisel #2 in Fig. 4.5 to turn a narrow groove.

Fig. 4.9. Use of chisel #3 in Fig. 4.5 to form a slightly concave section. This section was turned by using both chisel #3 and chisel #4.

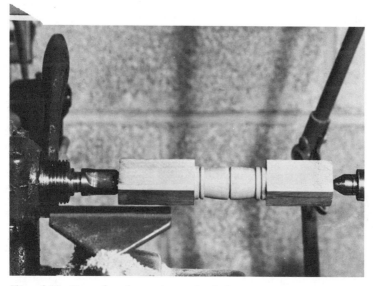

Fig. 4.10. Completed turning which has a square section on each side.

the steady rest, which should be set close to the work. Figures 4.6, 4.7, 4.8, and 4.9 show three turning chisels in use. Fig. 4.10 shows the completed section of the turning. When you are turning a long slender leg, there is a tendency for the wood to vibrate because of its natural elasticity. This leaves the surface rough. This can be minimized but not completely eliminated by keeping the cutting edges of the chisels very sharp. Final surfaces can be finished with a file and sandpaper. Final sanding must be done with very fine sandpaper to get rid of scratches.

Before attempting to turn a leg, you should practice some turning. Start with a softwood such as pine. Then graduate to hardwoods. Experiment with the various chisels until you learn what you can do with them.

4.1.3. QUEEN ANNE LEGS

An interesting and graceful leg used on many pieces of old furniture is the Queen Anne leg, which is illustrated in Fig. 4.11. You should not attempt to construct a piece of furniture with this type of leg until you have developed some skill in woodworking. However, these legs are not as difficult to make as they appear.

Start with a piece of wood 2½″ square. The piece should be accurately square. Its length should be that of the finished leg. If you have a lathe, locate the centers of both ends and drill center holes with the center point drill.

To form the shape of the leg, reproduce Fig. 4.12 full scale on a piece of cardboard. The vertical lines are spaced ½″ apart, the horizontal lines 1″ apart. These lines form a grid on which you can trace the contour of the leg, as indicated in the figure. When the drawing is completed, cut on the lines of the contour with a sharp knife to obtain a pattern for your wood. Trace the outline of the

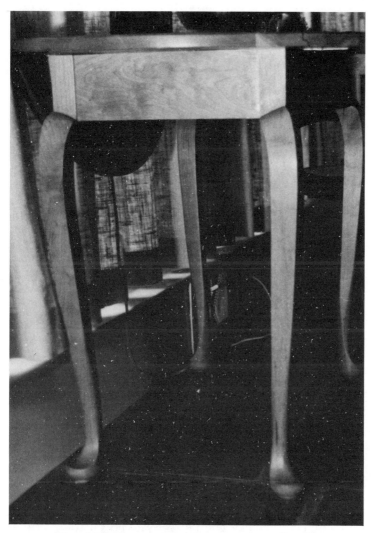

Fig. 4.11. Queen Anne legs on a small table.

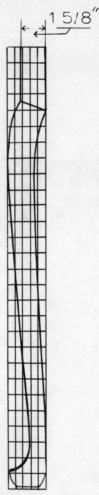

Fig. 4.12. Pattern for a Queen Anne leg.

pattern on the stock. The pattern should be traced right-side-up on sides A and C of Fig. 4.13. It should be turned over for tracing on side B and the side opposite side A. You should make the straight cuts at the top end of the leg with a hand saw. Cut along the curved portion of the pattern with a band saw or a hand coping-saw. Figure 4.14 shows a sample of a leg at this point in the process.

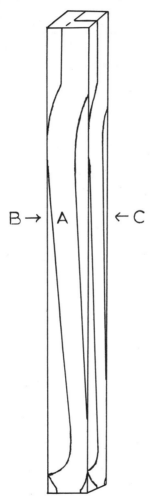

Fig. 4.13. Placement of the pattern on the square stock for a Queen Anne leg.

If you have a lathe, mount the leg in the lathe with the bottom end at the tailstock, turn the short pad at the bottom, and then form the bottom end in an approximate hemisphere. If you do not have a lathe, you will have to form the end by filing it to shape with a wood rasp and file. It is helpful to cut out and use a paper form as a gauge for this operation. The first set of Queen Anne legs I made were too long for my lathe, and I had to form the ends by hand. The rest of the job is strictly a hand operation. Use a coarse wood rasp and finish first with a file and finally sandpaper. You should carry through this operation on all four legs at the same time so that you can make them as like as possible. Depend on your eye to achieve a gracefully finished shape.

The Queen Anne legs on the small table shown in Fig. 4.11 were made from the pattern shown in Fig. 4.12. The roughly cut sample shown in Fig. 4.14 was to be used on this table, but it had to be discarded because of flaws in the wood which were not evident before it was cut out.

The pattern shown in Fig. 4.12 can be adapted to different heights by varying the vertical scale and the length of the straight portion of the top.

4.1.4. FLUTED LEGS

Fluted legs are first turned to a pattern. They have a section, usually of varying radius, on which the flutings are to be cut. If the flutings are to be cut by hand, this must be done with a V-shaped wood-carving chisel. Mark off on the circumference of the leg the number of flutings to be cut. Draw in longitudinal lines indicating the center of each fluting. The flutings are then carefully cut with the chisel and hand-sanded to the proper shape. This is a tedious job, but it can be done.

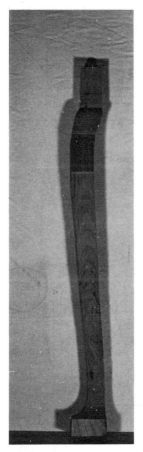

Fig. 4.14. Queen Anne leg cut out roughly with a band saw before it is finally formed to shape.

I have, on one occasion, built a pair of Sheraton banquet tables with fluted legs. I made use of a metal-turning lathe with a screw and micrometer scale to position it. I used a 60° thread-cutting bit oriented 90° to its normal cutting position. After marking off on the circumference of the leg the positions of its flutings, I planed out V-grooves to the proper depth, always working away from the largest diameter toward the smaller diameters and adjusting the micrometer to obtain the same depth of cut over the entire length of the fluting. This is a slow process, since it is not possible to make a very deep cut on each sweep of the bit. The result was a set of V-shaped flutings which were flat on top. I rounded them by working the edges down with sandpaper. Figure 4.15 shows the legs made in this way. It took hours of patient work to make the ten legs necessary, but they are beautiful and worth the effort.

Fig. 4.15. Sheraton banquet table with fluted legs.

4.2. MOLDINGS

Molding stock can often be purchased in convenient lengths.

It is possible to make moldings by using molding cutters on a table saw or drill press. For either of these tools it is necessary to purchase a molding-cutter head. A variety of molding-cutter bits is available for use with the heads. The manual supplied with a table saw will give you instructions for cutting a cove molding with a saw. It is possible to make large moldings by making cuts with more than one shape of cutter bit, combining such cuts with a cove cut made with the saw.

Detailed instructions for cutting moldings are supplied in the tool manuals. There is almost no limit to the number of molding shapes you can make with combinations of different molding-cutter heads.

4.3 BENDING

There are many times when it is necessary to bend a piece of lumber. The professional way to do it is to soak the piece and bend it around a hot bending-iron. The iron should not be so hot that it scorches the wood, but it should be well above the boiling point of water. As the wood is slowly forced into contact with the iron, the water turns to steam, which penetrates the wood and softens it so that it will bend without breaking. The wood should be left in contact with the iron until it is dry.

The amateur usually does not have bending-irons. It is not too difficult to bend most lumber if it is ¼″ thick or less. It should be soaked or cooked in boiling water and clamped on wooden forms until dry. Needless to say, straight-grained lumber must be selected for such parts. I have built dulcimers of walnut and cherry and had no great difficulty in bending the ⅛″ pieces for the sides after soaking them overnight in water at room temperature.

4.4. DRAWERS

A drawer may be designed with a front the same size as the opening so that it will be flush with the front of a cabinet. Or it may be designed to have a lip which overlaps the front. If the drawer does not have such a lip, the fit of the front in the opening must be accurate; any error in the fit will be obvious. If the drawer has a lip, the fit of the front in the opening is usually made with less care not only because it will not show but also because there is less danger of the drawer sticking during damp weather.

Nearly all drawers are assembled with dovetail joints. Figure 4.16 shows the dovetail joint for drawer fronts both with and without a lip. The method of making dovetail joints is covered in Section 3.2.4. Usually the drawer front is cut from ¾″ stock, the sides and back from ½″ stock. The dovetails are then cut ½″ long so they will be hidden at the front but extend all the way through the stock at the back. If the drawer has a lip, the lip is usually ¼″ thick so the dovetail will extend up to the lip, as indicated in Fig. 4.16.

After the dovetail tenons have been cut, the location of the mortises should be marked very carefully with a sharp pencil so that the bottoms of the sides and back will be flush with the bottom of the front.

The drawer bottom is usually made from ¼″ plywood mounted in a slot which has been cut in the sides, back, and front, as shown in Fig. 4.17.

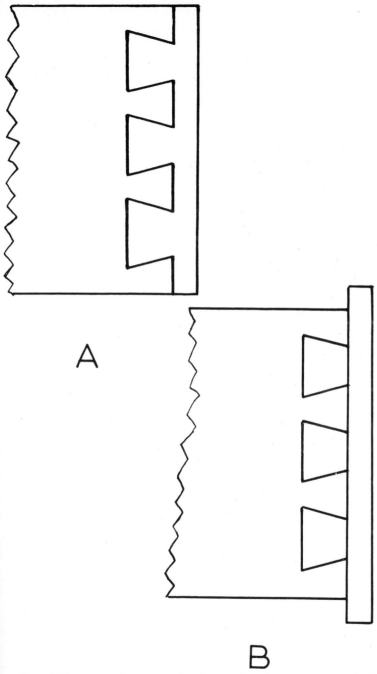

A

B

Fig. 4.16. Dovetail joint at the front of a drawer. A is a flush drawer and B is a drawer with a lip.

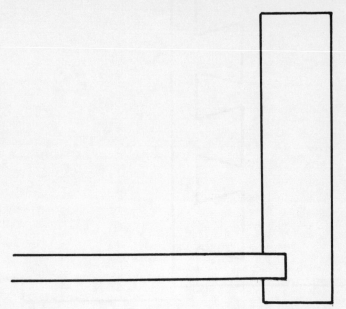

Fig. 4.17. Method of mounting a drawer bottom.

The sides and back of the drawer may be made from the same kind of lumber as the rest of the piece of furniture. In most instances they are made from white pine.

When all of the parts are complete, the drawer should be assembled without glue and tested in the place where it will be used, so that you will be certain it fits. The order of assembly is: 1), the front and one side, 2) the back, 3) the bottom, and 4) the second side. It is worthwhile to cut the bottom piece accurately, since this will assure the drawer's being square when it is clamped after gluing.

4.5. DRAWER RUNNERS AND DUST SHIELDS

The care with which drawer runners are made will de-

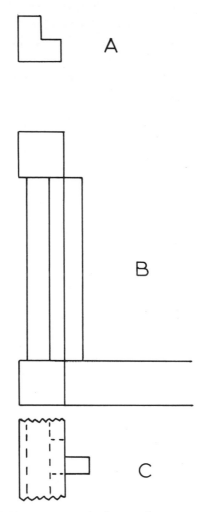

Fig. 4.18. A drawer runner. A shows the runner before it is installed. B shows a top view of the drawer runner installed. C shows a front view of the drawer runner installed.

termine how smoothly the drawers slide. I usually make drawer runners of hard maple. If that is not available, I use cherry. Softwood such as pine should not be used because the wear on drawer runners is severe.

Figure 4.18 A shows a drawer runner for a piece of furniture with corner posts. Figures 4.18 B and C show top and front views indicating how the runner is mounted. If the grain of the wood in the side of the piece of furniture runs vertically, the runner should not be glued in place because its grain will be perpendicular to that of the sides and this could cause the sides to crack if they shrink appreciably in dry weather. In such cases, runners should be mounted by means of screws countersunk in their side flanges; screw holes should be drilled oversize to allow motion of the screw as the wood changes dimensions with humidity.

If the piece of furniture does not have corner posts, the sides of the drawers will slide along the inside surface of the sides of the cabinet. The drawer runner, instead of being L-shaped like that shown in Fig. 4.18 A, will be a flat piece of the same thickness as the drawer separator in front. It is important to align the drawer runners very accurately to insure the drawer front's not getting cocked in the opening.

If the drawer front has a lip, the lip will serve as a stop when the drawer is closed. If the drawer does not have a lip, it will be necessary to install stops at the back so that it will close exactly flush with the front of the piece of furniture. These stops are simply blocks of wood glued to the back so that they will stop the drawer correctly.

Furniture such as dressers should have dust shields separating the drawers. The easiest way to install these is to cut a ¼″ slot about ¼″ deep in the edges of the drawer runners and the separators. Slide a sheet of ¼″ plywood into these slots from the rear before the back is installed. Installing these plywood sheets will be easier if the slots are cut slightly oversize. A few spots of glue in the slot will prevent the sheets from rattling.

5

Sharpening Tools

5.1 INTRODUCTION

Tools used to cut wood should be very sharp if they are to do their job effectively. Wood will dull tools quite rapidly. For example, a carbon-steel cutter bit in a metal-turning lathe will grow dull more quickly from turning wood than from turning metal. When a tool is dull, it does not cut the wood cleanly. Hardwoods will be much more likely to splinter and chip under a dull tool.

High-speed tools such as power saw blades, jointer blades, and turning chisels will grow hot if they are dull. If a tool is used after it has become slightly dull, its edge will wear away more rapidly. This is especially true of high-speed cutting tools probably because of the excess heat generated at the cutting edge. Wood-cutting tools are affected more than metal-cutting tools because wood does not conduct heat away as effectively.

5.2. PLANE BLADES

A plane blade with its chip breaker is mounted in the frame of the plane in the attitude (relative to the wood surface being planed) indicated in Fig. 5.1. The lower edge of the blade is ground on a circular grinding wheel, as shown in Fig. 5.2. Because the wheel is circular, the surface being ground will be "hollow ground." The wheel

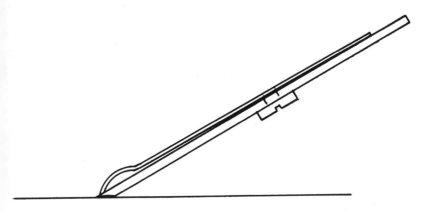

Fig. 5.1. Cutting attitude of a plane blade with its chip breaker. The hollow grind on the bevel of the blade is exaggerated
in this figure.

should be about 6″ to 8″ in diameter to produce the correct "hollow ground" surface. In order to hold the cutting edge straight, the chip breaker is usually turned at
right angles to the blade and the screw tightened so that
when it is pushed against the guide in front of the wheel
the surface being ground will contact the wheel as indicated in Fig. 5.2. The blade should be positioned so
that the "hollow ground" bevel will be about 3/16″ wide.
The blade is ground by moving it constantly from side
to side so that its cutting edge will be straight and square.
Grinding is continued until the ground surface extends up
to the cutting edge of the blade. As the ground surface
nears the cutting edge, great care must be exercised to
avoid burning. Cool the blade frequently by dipping it in
a pan of water. If the steel turns black, you will know
you have burned it. Burning the steel draws the temper

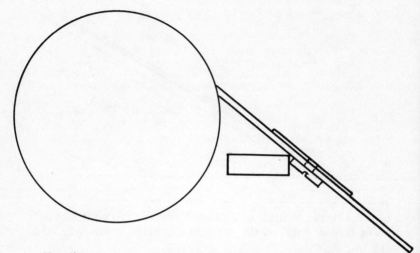

Fig. 5.2. Attitude of a plane blade being sharpened on a grinding wheel. The width of contact of the bevel of the blade with the wheel is about 3/16″. Note how the chip breaker screw-head is held against the guide on the grinder.

so it becomes soft and will not hold an edge.

When the grinding is completed, the edge of the blade will be rough on top. The next step is to hone the blade on a fine Carborundum stone. Position the blade on the stone so that the two sides of the bevel are in contact with the stone as indicated in Fig. 5.3. Holding the blade firmly at this angle, hone it with a circular motion. Honing is completed by turning the blade over and holding it nearly parallel to the stone and taking two or three strokes to remove metal turned over at the edge. Some machine oil should be applied to the stone to prevent it from filling up with metal particles. The chip breaker must be removed before honing. When it is replaced, its edge should be moved as close to the cutting edge of the blade as possible. However, be very careful not to push it over the newly sharpened edge because this will spoil its keenness.

When the blade becomes slightly dull with use, the sharp edge can be restored by being honed again on the Carborundum stone. It is not necessary to regrind the blade until it has been honed so many times that most of the "hollow ground" has disappeared or the edge of the blade has been nicked. You should form the habit of laying the plane on its side because nicks are nearly

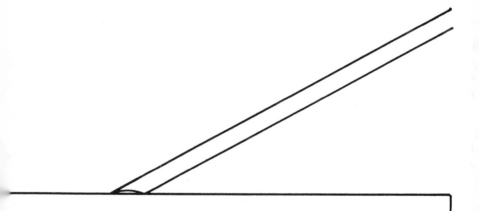

STONE

Fig. 5.3. Attitude of a plane blade while it is being honed on a Carborundum stone. The hollow grind on the bevel of the blade is exaggerated in this figure.

always caused by setting it down on a nail or screw or a tool.

A block plane should be sharpened in the same way. Since its blade is thinner, the "hollow ground" bevel should be about ⅛″ wide. Note that a block plane blade does not have a chip breaker and that it is installed in the plane with the bevel up instead of down. A chip breaker is not necessary in a block plane because the block plane is designed for use across the end grain of the wood.

5.3. CHISELS

A Chisel is ground and honed in the same way as a plane blade. Because a chisel is thicker, it is usually ground with a "hollow ground" bevel about ¼″ wide. With a little practice, you can learn to use your finger as a stop against the guide on the grinder to form the proper bevel. When using a chisel, you should have your Carborundum stone near at hand so that you can touch up the edge as it becomes dull.

5.4. POWER SAW BLADES

Many amateurs prefer to take their saw blades to a professional for sharpening. Blades with carbide tips can be used for a long time before they grow dull; they must be returned to the manufacturer for sharpening.

Some saw blades are called "flat ground" or "tapered." This means they are thicker at the teeth than in the body of the blade. The teeth in such saws are not set and will therefore make very smoothly finished cuts, but they should not be used for rough cuts. Blades used for rough cutting have the teeth set so that they are bent slightly

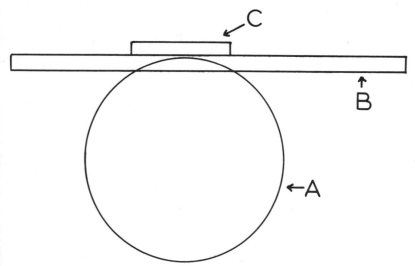

Fig. 5.4. Arrangement for trueing the circumference of a power saw blade with a Carborundum stone on the table. A is the saw blade, B is the saw table, and C is the Carborundum stone.

away from the plane of the blade. Alternate teeth are bent in opposite directions from the plane of the blade. The set in the teeth allows the saw to cut wider slots.

If you choose to do the sharpening, you should provide yourself with two discs of ¾″ plywood, each with a radius of about 1″ less than that of the saw blade, and with a bolt hole through the center. Clamp the saw blade between the discs by means of a bolt and nut. Clamp the assembly in a vise. File the teeth with a tapered triangular file, keeping the same angle on the bevel as it was originally.

After the saw has been filed two or three times, it will be necessary to true the blade before filing again. Figure 5.4 shows the arrangement for trueing the blade. A is the saw blade mounted in its normal position on the arbor. B is the saw table. C is a coarse Carborundum stone. First, lower the saw below the top of the table. While it is running, raise it very slowly until it contacts the Carborundum stone. Continue the process until all of the teeth have contacted the stone. The saw should be stopped and inspected frequently to avoid grinding away more of the tooth ends than necessary. Then file all the teeth until they come to a point.

If the saw blade is one in which the teeth are set, they should be reset after filing. In order to do this you will need a setting jig, which you can purchase. Instructions for use of the setting jig will be included with it. Do not attempt to set a saw without such a jig. Unless you do a great deal of woodwork, it is probably best to use a carbide-tipped saw for all rough work and to have a professional file your tapered blades used for finishing.

Each time a saw is filed, the teeth will be shortened. You should therefore cut back into the blade between the teeth with your file to retain approximately the original tooth length. If the bottom of the space between the teeth is round, a rattail file should be used.

5.5 WOOD BITS

Figure 5.5 shows the cutting end of a wood bit. It has: A) two circumferential cutters, which cut the circumference of the hole; B) two chisel cutters, which remove the wood from the center of the hole; and C) a screw, which draws the bit into the wood. The circumferential cutters and the chisel cutters occasionally need to be sharpened. Do this with a file. The circumferential cutters must be filed on the inside, never on the outside. The chisel cutters must be filed on the lower edge, as

Fig. 5.5. The cutting end of a wood bit. A is the circumferential cutter, B is the chisel cutter, and C is the screw which draws the bit into the wood.

the bit is viewed in Fig. 5.5, never on the top edge. If the circumferential cutters are filed on the outside edge, their effective cutting radius will be reduced and the bit will bind in the hole. If the chisel cutters are filed on the top edge, the cutting edges will not contact the wood quickly enough and will simply slide around on the surface without cutting.

You must be careful, when using a wood bit, to avoid striking metal. If you strike metal with the screw, there is not much you can do to repair the damage. Do not file the cutters, especially those with small bits, more than is absolutely necessary; removal of much of the metal will ruin the bit. The same amount of metal should be removed from the cutters on both sides of the bit if it is to operate symmetrically.

Twist drills can only be sharpened on a Carborundum wheel. You should not attempt to grind them unless you have a grinding jig. Grinding such drills so that the two lips are symmetrical takes skill. If the lips are not perfectly symmetrical, the bit will not drill a hole on center. If you purchase a drill-grinding jig, adequate instructions for its use will be included.

The bits used in mortising tools do not have a lead screw. The cutters on such bits are sharpened in the same way as those on regular wood bits.

5.6. JOINTER BLADES

Jointer blades can be sharpened only with a special jig. Such a jig can be purchased for use on a table saw. A special Carborundum wheel is used which fits on the saw arbor. After the blades are ground, great care must be exercised in mounting them in the arbor of the jointer. First, set the depth-of-cut scale on the jointer to zero. By a slow process of cut and try, adjust the blade as indicated in Fig. 5.6. Use the steel scale from a combination square. Adjust both ends of each of the three blades so that they barely touch the scale as the arbor is turned for the edge of the blade to pass through its highest point.

The table on the right in Fig. 5.6 is the one lowered to adjust the depth of cut. Before starting to adjust the blades in the joiner, check the adjustment of the table on the left by setting the depth of cut to zero and by placing a straight edge such as a large square on the right-hand table and, without turning the arbor, pushing a portion of the straight edge over the left-hand table. The straight edge should just touch this table. If it does not,

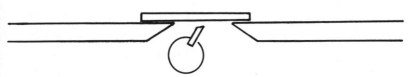

Fig. 5.6. Method of alignment of the cutter blades on a jointer with the jointer tables.

adjust the left-hand table until it just touches the straight edge.

When the blades are mounted in the jointer, they should be honed occasionally with a small Carborundum stone to keep the edges very sharp. Figure 5.7 shows how this is done. Use a sharpening stone about ¼″ wide, place it flat on the bevel of the blade, and rub it back and forth over the length of the blade. Be careful not to let your fingers project below the stone on the side of the sharp edge of the blade because you can get a nasty cut.

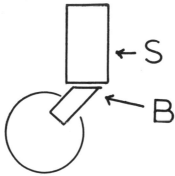

Fig. 5.7. Method of honing a jointer blade. B is the jointer blade. S is the sharpening stone. The normal jointer has three blades, but only one of the blades is shown here.

5.7. HAND SAWS

The teeth on a hand saw are sharpened with a file.
Filing a hand saw should not be attempted by an amateur unless he can learn the process under the supervision of a professional. Great accuracy must be used to
file and set the teeth or the saw will follow a curve instead of a straight line. If a saw is handled carefully in
the shop, it does not need to be sharpened very often.
The amateur will do well to take his saw to a professional
when it needs resharpening.

6

Factors Involved in Assembling A Piece of Furniture

6.1. SANDING PRIOR TO ASSEMBLY

Although final sanding is always necessary after a piece of furniture is assembled, much labor can be saved if individual parts are sanded prior to assembly. When the lumber has been planed to dimensions in a planing mill, it is moved over rotating planing-blades which make it slightly like a washboard. This usually is not immediately obvious. It becomes obvious as soon as you start to sand the surface, because the sandpaper initially contacts only its high points. Individual parts should be sanded until all saw marks, bruises, and the washboard effect are eliminated. Starting with a medium grade sandpaper and finish with fine sandpaper. Avoid dropping the parts or striking them with tools.

If you have a power-belt sander, you can sand the individual parts with it, using a sandpaper belt labeled "fine." Avoid taking off more wood than necessary and thereby spoiling the fit of the parts. Do not attempt to do this with the rotary sanding attachment which is available for use with small hand drills; it will gouge the lumber regardless of how careful you are. I have found very few instances in which such a device can be satisfactory.

After sanding with a power-belt sander, you should always finish off with hand sanding. There is an important difference between the two actions. The belt on a belt sander runs continuously in one direction, while in hand sanding you move the block back and forth. With some woods, particularly walnut, the belt sander causes the ends of the grain to curl up, leaving a fuzzy surface. The back-and-forth action of a hand sanding block assures that these ends will be cut off.

Normally sanding is done parallel to the grain in order to avoid scratches. However, there is one exception to this. When you glue a panel or table top, the unit will not be flat, no matter how carefully you have matched the pieces and clamped them together. You can correct this by sanding across the grain with medium grade sandpaper. In extreme cases, you can plane across the grain with a hand plane. When you have obtained a flat surface, sand it parallel to the grain until all scratches from cross-grain sanding or planing are removed.

Hand sanding should be done with the sandpaper in a block which has a soft backing for the sandpaper. It is possible to purchase a sandpaper holder with a felt pad backing up the sandpaper. Small areas can be sanded by using your thumb or fingers to back up small pieces of sandpaper. The amount of sanding which can be done in this manner is limited because blisters form on your fingers quite rapidly from the heat generated by the process.

6.2. GLUE

There are three types of glue available for gluing furniture. All are good. Your choice depends on the particular application.

6.2.1. HIDE OR FLAKE GLUE

This type of glue has been in use for several hundred

years. It was used on all antique furniture. Its holding quality is demonstrated by the number of pieces of furniture in which the joints are still sound after more than a hundred years.

Hide glue is obtained in the form of hard flakes which must be dissolved in water for use. Since this glue must be applied hot, it is necessary to have a "glue pot." This can be made by mounting a small can within a larger one to form a double boiler. The inner can, in which the glue is heated, should be either heavily plated or made of aluminum; bare iron or steel will discolor the glue. An aluminum beer can with the top cut out is satisfactory. It is possible to purchase electrically-heated glue pots.

To prepare the glue, put some of the flakes in the inner container and add just enough water to·cover them. Allow them to soak overnight. The flakes will become soft by absorbing just about the amount of water needed to produce the proper consistency. Pour off any excess water. Heat in the double boiler to about 180°F (82°C). *Do not boil the glue!* The consistency of the glue should be about that of medium grade automobile-cylinder oil. Great care must be exercised to maintain the glue at the correct temperature and consistency. If the glue is too thick, more water should be added. If it is too thin, make up more glue with less water and combine the two mixtures. A batch of glue used on a previous job can be reheated for use. The number of reheatings should be limited to three or four because each reheating causes some loss of strength in the glue.

The parts to be glued should be warmed to a temperature between 80° and 90° F (27° to 32° C) as you work with them. If a large piece of furniture is to be glued, it is practically necessary for you to work in a hot room of high humidity and to work very rapidly.

It is obviously difficult for an amateur to do a good

job with this kind of glue. Its important property is that it can be softened with water, which enables you to take joints apart without injuring the wood. If, for example, you were to make a violin, you would need to use this kind of glue to be able to take the glued joints apart to repair it.

6.2.2. PLASTIC RESIN GLUE

Plastic resin glue is purchased in the form of a powder which can be dissolved in cold water and used at room temperature. Mix it with water just before use. Add a little water at a time. Stirring vigorously until the mixture attains the consistency of thick cream. Because it will not keep, only that amount which will be used in a particular operation should be mixed. However, be sure to mix enough to do the entire job. Delaying to mix an additional batch will permit the glue which has already been applied to start setting.

This is an easy kind of glue to use. But its setting, unlike that of the hide glue, involves a nonreversible polymerization process, which means it can not be softened after it is set. The kinds of plastic resin glues normally used will not be adversely affected by moderate exposure to water. Continuous exposure to water as in the case of boats or outdoor furniture will cause the glue to deteriorate. For such applications special water-resistant plastic resin glues are available.

Containers of this powder must be kept tightly closed because the powder will absorb moisture from the atmosphere and deteriorate. I prefer to purchase this glue in small containers.

There are several brands of this glue available. Carefully follow the directions on the container. I use this glue for nearly all new furniture.

6.2.3. WHITE GLUE

The easiest glue to use is the white glue which is available, ready to use, in squeeze bottles.

This is a strong glue which sets to a hardness about equal to that of wood. It is always immediately available. It is particularly useful for regluing loose joints in old furniture because the entire space in the joint can be filled with the glue, which hardens without shrinking. Also, it sets in about thirty minutes, although it does not attain full strength until about thirty-six hours after application. I always keep a bottle of this glue at hand.

6.3. CLAMPS AND JIGS

Nearly every piece of furniture will require four bar clamps to be properly clamped together when it is glued. I have found that clamps which use a length of ¾″ pipe for the bar are very satisfactory. If you contemplate gluing a piece of furniture, I would advise the purchase of four sets of these clamps. You can purchase the necessary lengths of pipe, threaded on both ends, from your plumber. The lengths most commonly needed are 2′ and 4′. However, it is not desirable to use an excessive length of pipe for any particular job because the weight of excess pipe projecting beyond the work may pull it out of shape. It is best therefore to purchase the lengths as they are needed.

I have equipped the shoes of my clamps with permanent wood blocks by drilling two holes in each shoe and attaching the blocks with roundhead wood screws. It is important to protect the wood with wood blocks, which prevent damage to the surface by the shoe. If you do not fasten the blocks to the shoes, you will need more than two hands to apply the clamp and at the same time hold the blocks in place.

You will eventually need several C clamps in 2", 4", and 6" sizes. I do not advocate the purchase of a large number of these clamps immediately. They represent a considerable investment. It is best to purchase them as they are needed.

You will find some instances in which jigs will be required to hold something in shape while it is being glued and clamped. You should have some fir plywood available to fabricate such jigs as they are needed.

6.4. ORDER OF ASSEMBLY

Nearly every piece of furniture is a rectangle with two end sections joined by one or two stringers on the back and front. Normally the ends are glued first. Then, when the glue has set, they are joined by gluing in the front and back stringers.

Usually two clamps are needed to hold the ends while the glue sets. Four are needed to hold the assembly when the front and back stringers are glued in. Some tables have stringers only at the top. Such pieces will require only one clamp for the ends and two clamps for the final assembly. Clamps must always be applied so that they exert their force directly in line with the stringers. If you apply the clamp between the stringers, the legs will be bowed and will remain that way after the clamps are removed.

6.5. DRY RUNS

Before gluing any section of a piece of furniture, a complete dry run should be made without glue but including clamping. When the section is clamped together, check to be certain that it fits squarely. If it does not, a jig may be required to hold it to the desired shape while the glue is setting. Such a dry run will insure not only that the parts fit together but that all necessary clamps and jigs are at hand before you start gluing. Since all types of glue begin to set in a few minutes after application, it is important for everything to be ready before you use it.

6.6. GLUING

You have carefully made a dry run of assembling the unit which you are about to glue. All necessary clamps and jigs are at hand. The glue is ready. The glue can be applied to the inside surfaces of the mortises by means of a small wooden paddle. Do not put an excess of glue in the mortises; it will squeeze out when the joint is fitted together. Simply coat the inside surfaces with a thin layer. The tenons can be coated in the same manner. Or you can use a small brush of a type tinners use to apply soldering flux. As soon as all surfaces are coated, push the joints together and apply the clamps, turning them up firmly but not tightly enough to distort the structure. As soon as the clamping is complete, take a clean rag, dip it in warm water, and carefully wash off any glue which has been squeezed out of the joints.

Some kinds of glue are supposed to set within thirty minutes to four hours. The wise thing to do is leave the unit in the clamps overnight.

If you use a brush to apply the glue, wash it out as soon as you finish washing away the excess glue. If you mixed plastic resin glue in a container, discard any remaining glue and wash the container. It is easy to wash out the glue with warm water while it is still fluid but difficult to dig out after it solidifies. If you forget to wash the brush before the glue dries on it, you may as well throw it in the trash.

7
Sanding and Finishing

7.1. FINAL SANDING OF THE ASSEMBLED PIECE

Part of the process of gluing, as described in the previous chapter, is to wash away excess glue from the joints. Note that water raises the grain of wood so that it becomes rough. This roughness must be removed by sanding. This should be done with 3/0 sandpaper. All areas must be carefully examined to be certain that no glue is left in the surface of the wood. You may find spots away from the joints touched by your fingers which had picked up a small amount of glue. All of this must be removed. Even a small amount of glue in the surface of the wood will affect any finish. You may find some areas in which you will have to scrape the surface in order to be certain that the glue is entirely removed. After scraping and sanding with 3/0 sandpaper, finish by sanding the entire structure with 6/0 sandpaper to obtain the final smoothness. When you think the surface is perfect, wipe it carefully with a cotton rag and inspect it under a good light. Any area which shows imperfections should be worked over with sandpaper until they are removed. Remember that these imperfections will be more obvious after finishing than before. After sanding is completed, carefully wipe off all dust with a clean cotton rag. Other kinds of rags shed lint. The final wiping should be done with a tack rag.

7.2. STAIN

In some instances it may be desirable to stain the wood. There is a variety of water-soluble and oil-soluble stains available. If you wish to change the color of the wood, one of these stains can be applied. The usual method of application is to apply the stain to the surface with a brush and then to rub off the excess with a rag. More applications are made until the desired depth of color is attained. There are many people who believe that mahogany should be red because that is its traditional stain. If you belong to that school, you will want to stain your mahogany pieces with red mahogany oil-stain. I happen to prefer most wood in its natural color—even mahogany, which finishes to a beautiful brown when not stained.

It is not necessary to use a quality brush to apply the stain. It is necessary to clean the brush to remove both pigment and oil. If an oil stain was used, clean the brush with five or six washings in turpentine, wash with soap and water, and finish by thoroughly rinsing. If a water-soluble stain was used, no rinsing with turpentine is necessary. After cleaning, the brush should be hung up to dry, bristles down.

7.3. WOOD FILLER

New furniture implies the use of new wood. The surface of wood differs from that of metals or plastics in that it is not continuous. It consists of a mass of fibers with spaces between them. To achieve a good finish, you must fill these spaces in the surface to form as nearly as possible a continuous surface.

Wood with large spaces between the fibers is called open-or coarse-grained wood. Wood with small spaces between the fibers is called fine-grained. Walnut is more open-grained than cherry or maple.

The grain of the wood may be filled by means of a finish or by a special filler used before the finish is applied.

The most common kind of filler is called paste wood-filler. It consists of very finely powdered inert material saturated with a drying oil. When it is purchased, the solid material nearly fills the container, with a shallow layer of oil on top. In order to use this material to fill the grain of wood, it is necessary to remove some of the solid material, place it in a separate container, and dilute it with linseed oil and turpentine. The mixture should be worked with a wooden paddle until the solid material is in complete suspension in the liquid.

The solid material in the paste wood-filler is white. Used directly on a dark wood, it whitens all of the spaces between the wood fibers—an undesirable effect. It is necessary therefore to add oil pigment to the mixture to bring it to the color of the wood. Remember that dark wood appears much lighter before a finish is applied than after. In order to judge the color, take a scrap of the wood, sand it, apply some linseed oil, and match to it the color of your filler.

Turkey Burnt Umber will match most walnut, but some walnut has a reddish tinge; thus a small amount of Burnt Sienna may also be necessary. Mahogany and cherry will require Burnt Sienna with a small amount of Turkey Burnt Umber. In working with cherry, you should remember that the wood will develop more color as it ages and that the color of the filler should match aged cherry.

These pigments are sold in all paint shops. Since a small amount of pigment will produce a lot of color, use it sparingly and be certain that all of the pigment is dispersed in the mixture.

When the filler is made up to the proper color, its consistency should be about that of varnish. Be sure to make up enough filler to do the entire job, since it is not easy to match colors.

Apply filler liberally with an inexpensive brush. Allow it to stand until the surface becomes dull. Then rub it across the grain of the wood with cotton rags, which will rapidly soak up the oil. Final rubbing should be done with a clean rag. When you are finished, wash your hands, take a clean cloth, and wipe the entire surface carefully to avoid leaving permanent fingerprints.

Caution. Hang up all oil-soaked rags to dry. Do not wad them up, since oxidation of the oil may generate enough heat to ignite them and cause a fire.

The filler should be allowed to dry for forty-eight hours. The surface should then be rubbed, with the grain, with #00 steel wool. All steel wool particles should be wiped away with a cloth. The surface should now be very smooth and ready for the final finish.

7.4. OIL FINISH

An oil finish may be applied with or without a previout application of filler. Linseed oil is diluted with one part of turpentine to about two parts of oil. The purpose of the turpentine is to help the oil penetrate the wood and to accelerate the drying of the oil. The mixture is applied generously to the surface with an inexpensive brush and allowed to soak into the wood for at least an hour. It is then rubbed with rags, at first across the grain and then with the grain. When all excess oil has been rubbed off the surface, wash your hands. Rub over the entire surface with a clean rag to be certain there are no oil fingerprints on it which will become permanent when the oil dries. Allow to dry for at least twenty-four hours. Repeat the process. After three coats have been applied, rub the surface lightly with #00 steel wool. Then use a mixture of equal parts of varnish, linseed oil, and turpentine for at least two additional coats.

When using the mixture with varnish, test the varnish to find out how long it takes to start getting sticky. When the varnish becomes sticky, you can not rub it.

If a filler was not used prior to the finishing, more coats of the varnish mixture will be required to fill the grain of the wood. When the surface acquires a satiny texture, it is satisfactory.

In applying an oil finish to a large piece, do not apply oil to too large an area at one time. Rubbing is hard work, and you may have given yourself a larger job than you can handle at one time.

You should always hang up the oil-soaked rags to dry to avoid danger of fire. You should also clean your brush.

7.5. SHELLAC FINISH

Shellac is a relatively easy finish to use. White shellac is the most usual, but there are some instances in which the brown color produced by orange shellac is desired.

Shellac is purchased as a solution in methyl (wood) alcohol. The solution is too highly concentrated to produce a good finish. It should be diluted with an equal amount of shellac thinner. Apply the shellac with a good quality hog-bristle brush. Brush it out well, but do not brush so long that you leave brush marks. After the first coat is dry, sand lightly with 6/0 sandpaper and repeat. If filler has been used, three coats should be sufficient. If filler has not been used, additional coats will be required to fill the grain of the wood with shellac.

After the last coat is dry, the surface can be rubbed

down to a satiny finish. Use a rag dipped in a mixture
of linseed oil and powdered pumice stone. Add only
enough oil to the pumice stone powder to serve as a
lubricant. When the rubbing is completed, wipe off all
of the oil, wash your hands, and wipe the entire surface again with a clean cloth to remove fingerprints.
The brush should be washed five or six times in small
amounts of clean shellac thinner and then in soap and
water. Rinse thoroughly with water to remove all of
the soap and hang it, bristles down, to dry.

Be careful in your use of shellac and shellac thinner.
Wood alcohol is very poisonous. Work in a well-venti-
lated area and avoid getting the shellac and the thinner
on your hands.

7.6. VARNISH FINISH

Varnish is applied in the same way as shellac. Only
a good quality hog-bristle varnish brush should be used.
Varnish requires a longer time to dry than shellac.
Therefore, unless you can work in a dust-free room, dust
will settle on the varnish before it dries and the result-
ing surface will be rough. Sand with 6/0 sandpaper before applying the next coat. If the wood has been filled,
three coats of varnish should be sufficient. If you want
a glossy finish, you will have to find a dust-free atmosphere in which to apply the last coat. However, if you
wish to have a rubbed-down finish, the last coat should
be rubbed down with linseed oil and powdered pumice
stone. This rubbing will remove all dust. The tech-
nique of rubbing down a varnished surface is the same
as that used on a shellacked surface, except that it takes
more work. I prefer a rubbed varnish finish to any other. Varnish is very durable, does not scratch easily, and
rubs down to a beautiful finish.

When the final rubbing is complete, wash your hands, and with a clean cloth wipe away fingerprints.

7.7. LACQUER FINISH

There are two types of finishing lacquer: spray lacquer and brushing lacquer. Lacquer consists of a plastic dissolved in a solvent. Unlike varnish, which is a resin dissolved in a drying oil, it dries by evaporation of the solvent; this leaves the plastic on and in the surface of the wood. The difference between spray lacquer and brushing lacquer is simply a difference in the rate of evaporation of the solvent.

Most of the brushing lacquers dry so rapidly that it is difficult to brush them out without leaving brush marks on the surface. It is possible to purchase spray lacquer in aerosol containers. Be sure to follow the directions on the container for application of the lacquer.

Most lacquers are considerably softer than varnish. They will scratch very easily. Since they are partially soluble in alcohol, a glass of an alcoholic beverage is likely to leave a ring on them. There is an alcohol-proof brushing lacquer also immune to water, which brushes out very well without leaving brush marks. This lacquer can also be exposed to considerable heat without damage.

Most lacquers can be rubbed down with linseed oil and powdered pumice stone if a satiny finish is desired.

7.8. FRENCH POLISH

French polish makes a beautiful finish, although its application requires a considerable amount of labor. The polish is a combination of linseed oil and shellac. A pad of cotton which can be compressed to a ball about 1″ in diameter is placed on the center of a piece of cotton fabric about 6″ square. Pour enough shellac on the cotton pad to make it slightly wet. Wrap the fabric around the pad to form a ball with the extra cloth forming a handle. Dip the ball lightly into a saucer of linseed oil. Use it to rub the surface of the wood. The oil serves as a lubricant. The shellac squeezes through the fabric and is rubbed into the grain of the wood. The process is continued, shellac being added as needed, the ball being dipped into oil whenever it becomes sticky, until the grain of the wood is filled with shellac. Although this finish requires a great deal of labor, especially with an open-grained wood such as walnut, it produces a very desirable finish.

7.9. ENAMEL FINISH

Painted furniture has always had important uses. Modern enamels are very good. There are many beautiful colors available. Modern furniture enamels are essentially varnishes containing opaque pigments.

The first coat should always be an enamel undercoat. After it has been allowed to dry, it should be rubbed down with steel wool because the undercoat causes some raising of the grain.

The enamel may have either a glossy or flat finish.

After the enamel undercoat has been rubbed down, one or two coats of the enamel should be applied with a good hog-bristle varnish brush. The enamel should be brushed out so that it will not run down and form ridges.

Enamel should be cleaned from the brush in the same way as varnish.

8

An Example

8.1. INTRODUCTION

In order to illustrate the various techniques involved in furniture construction, I will show step by step how I built two Canterburys designed originally by Sheraton for the Archbishop of Canterbury. The Canterbury was intended to be used as a music rack but will serve equally well as a book or magazine rack. According to Sheraton's design, the Canterbury can be constructed either with square legs tapered at the bottom or with turned legs. I constructed my two Canterburys simultaneously, one with square legs and one with turned legs. The one with square legs was made from walnut, the one with turned legs from cherry. Figure 8.1 shows these finished pieces.

The Canterbury is 18" long, 12" wide, and 20" high overall. It has three spacers, of which two are removable and the center one permanently fixed in place. It has a handle.

In order to be certain that all important details in the process were covered, I wrote this chapter step-by-step as I built the Canterburys.

8.2. THE LEGS

Both kinds of legs are 1⅛" square and 20" long. The first step therefore was to cut four cherry and four wal-

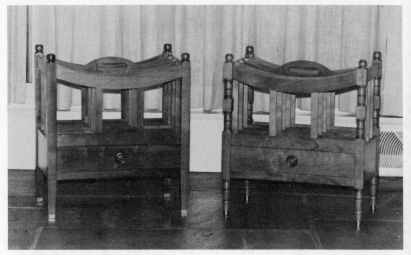

Fig. 8.1. The two Canterburys constructed by the author.

nut pieces, each 1⅛" square and 21" long. The extra inch of length was necessary in order to avoid a center hole —cut for turning—in the top of the leg. It was cut off as the last step in making the legs. Great care was exercised to make sure the legs were cut to precise 1⅛" squares. The ends were cut off squarely so that their cen-

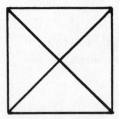

Fig. 8.2. Method of marking the ends of a square piece for location of center holes for the lathe centers.

ters could be accurately located when set in the lathe. To locate the centers, the ends of the legs were marked as indicated in Fig. 8.2. A center punch was driven in at the point of intersection of the lines. A center point drill provided a tapered hole to accomodate the lathe centers.

8.2.1. THE TURNED CHERRY LEGS

The first step was to mark the four cherry legs for turning. Figure 8.3 shows how they were marked. The crosshatched areas were turned. The areas not turned were left square. All areas except that between B and C are where mortise and tenon joints were to be made.

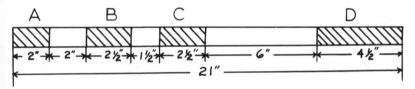

Fig. 8.3. Method of laying out a leg for turning. The cross-hatched areas are those to be turned to cylinders with the same diameter as the width dimension of the square leg.

Figure 8.4 shows the detail of the turning at A in Fig. 8.3, which is the top of the leg. Section A in Fig 8..4 is the square portion below the turning. The dotted line B is the line along which the stub was cut off when the turning was completed. This is the only turned portion on the walnut legs.

Figure 8.5 is a detail of the turnings at B and C in Fig. 8.3. The sections A and B in Fig. 8.5 are the square sections on each side of the turnings. Figure 8.6 is a de-

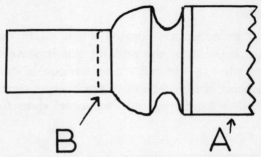

B   A

Fig. 8.4. Detail of the turning at the top of the leg. A is the square portion below the turning. The dotted line B shows where the stub will be cut off as the last step in making the leg. This turning is made on both the turned-leg and the square-leg Canterburys.

tail of the turning at D in Fig. 8.3. A is the square section above the turning. B is turned down to a smaller diameter to accept a brass cap. The original Sheraton design called for brass casters on the ends of the legs because the rack was intended to be pushed under the pianoforte. However, casters do not roll well on modern carpets. So I put a ½″ length of ¾″ brass tubing over B and blended it into the turned wood above B. The diameter of B was such that the tubing would fit snugly. It was glued in place with white plastic glue. The Canterbury is small enough so that it can be easily moved by the handle on top.

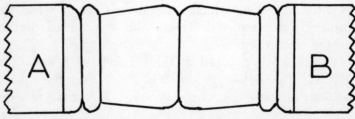

Fig. 8.5. Detail of the turnings at B and C of Fig. 8.3. The portions at A and B are the square portions above and below the turning.

8.2.2. THE SQUARE WALNUT LEGS

The square pieces of walnut were prepared for centering in the lathe in the same way as the cherry, and the top ends were turned as indicated in Fig. 8.4. The bottom ends of these legs, which correspond to section D in Fig. 8.3, were tapered from 1⅛" to ¾" square at the bottom end, following the procedure outlined in Section 4.1.1.

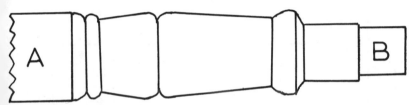

Fig. 8.6. Detail of the bottom turning of the turned legs. A is the square section above the turning. B is reduced in diameter to accept a piece of brass tubing as a decorative element at the bottom end of the leg.

8.3. THE END SECTIONS

Figure 8.7 shows the configuration of the ends of the Canterbury. The mortises in the legs were located from this figure. The stringers were cut from ½" lumber. Therefore the mortises and tenons were made ¼" wide. It was desirable that the outside edges of the stringers be ⅛" from the outside edges of the legs. Since ⅛" was to be removed from each side of the stringer to form the tenon, the edges of the mortises were located ¼" from the outside edges of the legs, as indicated in Fig. 8.8. A is the

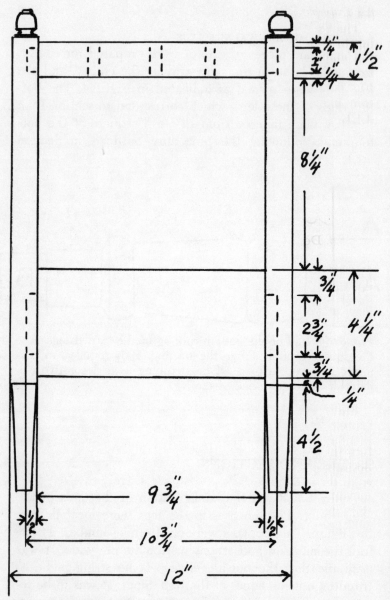

Fig. 8.7. Kind of sketch which should be made of each section of a piece of furniture before fabrication.

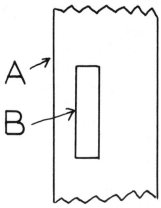

Fig. 8.8. Kind of sketch which should be used to illustrate the location of mortises in legs.

outside edge of the leg. B is the mortise.

When I am building a piece of furniture, I always make sketches similar to Figs. 8.7 and 8.8. I usually make them freehand. I do not worry about doing them to scale, but I always include the dimensions. This is an important safeguard against mistakes.

From Fig. 8.7 it is obvious that there are two stringers on each end, one 1½" wide and one 4¼" wide, both 10¾" long. We will therefore need two pieces of cherry and two pieces of walnut ½" thick and 1½" wide for the two Canterburys. We will also require corresponding pieces 4½" wide. In other words, we will need a total of eight pieces of two different widths cut to the same length. It is important that all four pieces for each Canterbury be of identical length. Attachments for the miter on a power saw are available which will help you achieve this exactitude. I used one—a stop adjusted so that it was 10¾" from the near edge of the saw blade. I placed each piece with its squared end against the stop and sawed it off.

The tenons are each ½″ long. So, in cutting them, I moved the stop to a point 10¼″ from the edge of the saw blade. I lowered the saw so that it would make a cut ⅛″ deep. I cut each piece on all the sides of each end without disturbing the setting of the stop. The cuts on the edges of the 1½″ pieces were to be ¼″ deep. Without disturbing the stop, I raised the saw so that it would make a cut ¼″ deep and made the cuts. Then I raised the saw to ¾″ and made the cuts on the 4¼″ stringers. By following this procedure I accurately aligned the shoulders on each of the stringers. The lengths from shoulder to shoulder on all of the stringers were equally precise.

The same thing can be accomplished with a miter box. Simply clamp a block to the base of the miter box to serve as a stop. If you do not have a table saw or a miter box, you will have to locate all these cuts by measure-

Fig. 8.9. Use of a mortising tool to make a mortise for the leg.

ment. Carefully mark the positions of all cuts. Make them with the small back saw.

The mortises were prepared according to the procedure outlined in Section 3.2.2. Excess wood around the tenons was removed with a chisel. Although Canterburys are small pieces of furniture, a total of fifty mortise and tenon joints was required for each. This should emphasize the importance of a mortising attachment for a drill press. Since I made the mortises with such a tool, Fig. 8.9 shows the tool as it was being used to make a mortise for one of the legs of the cherry Canterbury.

The three grooves cut in the top stringers to accomodate the separators divide the 9¾″ length between the legs into four equal parts, as indicated by the dotted lines in Fig. 8.7. They were cut ¼″ deep and ½″ wide. It was necessary to cut the grooves before the end sections were glued together.

8.4. THE FRONT AND BACK SECTIONS

The top stringers on the front and back sections as well as those on the separators are curved. In addition, the top stringer on the center separator has a handle. Since these parts as well as the back panel and the pieces which go above and below the drawer are all of the same length and have ½″ tenons on each end, they were cut according to the procedure described in Section 8.3. In this instance, the pieces were cut 16¾″ long. Figure 8.10 shows how the curved pieces were laid out for cutting. The piece which incorporates the handle was 3½″ wide. Those without the handle were 3⅛″ wide. The arrangement shown in Fig. 8.10 was laid out on a sheet of plywood. A beam compass was used to strike the arcs. The beam compass was made from a ¾″ square strip of

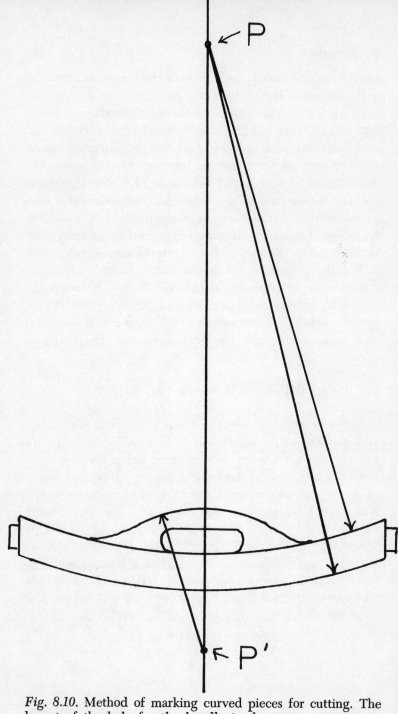

Fig. 8.10. Method of marking curved pieces for cutting. The layout of the hole for the handle in the center separator is also shown.

straight wood. Holes were drilled for a nail at point P in the beam compass and in the plywood. Two holes were drilled in the beam compass to fit a pencil, one 22⅞" from P, and the other 21⅜" from P. The five curved pieces for each Canterbury were all marked with this jig. In addition, the extra arc for the top of the handle was marked by the same method, with the beam compass set up for a 6" radius. The two circular arcs for the top of the center separator were blended, using a draftsman's flexible curve. The marked pieces were cut out on a band saw. Since the radius of curvature of the ends of the slot is quite small, it was not possible to cut this very accurately. Considerable wood had to be removed with a wood rasp and sandpaper.

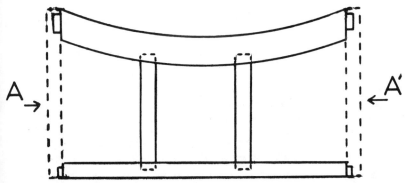

Fig. 8.11. Arrangement of the vertical strips in the front and back sections as well as in the separators. The dotted portion shows the arrangement of the end pieces on the separators.

There are two vertical strips between the bottom of the curved stringers and the top of the back panel and the top of the stringer over the drawer. These strips are ¾" wide and ¼" thick. Their ends are mortised in at the top and bottom. Figure 8.11 shows the arrangement of these strips.

8.5. GLUING THE MAIN ASSEMBLY

When the parts were completed to this point, the components of each of the end sections were carefully sanded and each end section was glued according to the procedure described in Section 6.6. Following this, the two end sections of each Canterbury were joined by means of the front and back parts. Plastic resin glue was used for all joints.

8.6. THE TOP

The top on which the separators rest was made from ½" lumber. I followed the procedure described in Section 3.2.6., except that I used no dowel pins in the glued joints because there would be no mechanical strain on them. The pieces glued together were about 1" longer than the top. Their combined widths were somewhat greater than the total width required.

When the glue was thoroughly dry, I roughly sanded to correct for any irregularity at the joints. I then cut and planed it to a width which would just pass between the top stringers. I squared one end and sanded it until the end grain was smooth. The amount of sanding required will depend on the saw used to make this cut. I used a tapered saw, which makes a smooth cut, and the end was easily finished with sandpaper. If the end is very ragged, you will have to plane it with a block plane and then finish it with 3/0 sandpaper. The block plane must be very sharp, especially if it is used to plane cherry. It should be set to make a very shallow cut, or it will gouge the surface. When the end was square and smooth, 1 cut notches for the legs.

It was now necessary to cut and square the other end by measurement. It was finally smoothed in the same way as the first. Fitting the top will teach you the importance of being certain that the assembly is square when it is glued.

8.7. THE DRAWER RUNNERS

The drawer runners were cut from $\frac{7}{8}''$ square stock. Figure 8.12 shows two views of the bottom drawer runners. Width A was made accurately equal to the distance from the end panel to the inside edge of the legs. Length B was equal to the distance between the legs. Length C was equal to the distance between the back panel and the stringer below the drawer.

These drawer runners were installed with three #8 wood screws $1\frac{1}{4}''$ long. They were mounted so that the surface on which the drawer glides was flush with the top of the stringer below the drawer. They were also mounted perpendicularly to the front legs, as determined by a try square. This was important if the drawer was to be flush with both the top and bottom stringers when it was closed. This would not be so important if the drawer had a lip.

In order to complete the drawer runners, it was necessary to provide two strips above the drawers. These strips serve a twofold purpose: 1) they provide a guide that keeps the drawer from tilting down when it is partially

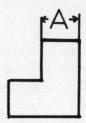

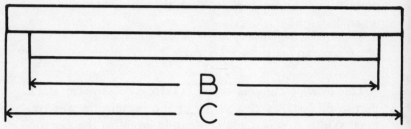

Fig. 8.12. Detail of the bottom drawer runners.

open; and 2) they serve as the means of attaching the top. The width of these strips was ⅞″, their thickness approximately ¼″. The top strips were mounted with screws similar to those used for the bottom drawer runners. After the holes were drilled and the strips mounted in place and tested for proper clearance, I removed the screws, applied white glue to the surface which contacts the end panel, and put the screws back in again. Glue was necessary if the strips were to hold the top with adequate strength.

When the drawer runners were all in place, the top was attached to the top drawer runners with three ¾″ #8 screws on each end. These screws were placed so that they would be covered by the three separators when they were installed.

8.8. THE DRAWER

The drawers used in these Canterburys are flush and were assembled with dovetail joints as described in Section 3.2.4. The drawer fronts are ¾″ thick, the sides and back are ½″ thick.

The drawer fronts are nominally 3″ by 15¾″. However, such drawer fronts must be planed to fit with enough slack so that they will not stick in damp seasons. If such a drawer is made during the summer, 1/32″ clearance is adequate. If it is made during the winter from lumber stored in a heated area, more clearance will be necessary. Since these Canterburys were made during the summer, the fronts were adjusted to provide about 1/32″ clearance.

The dovetail joints, where the sides of the drawers have been attached to the fronts, are hidden so that the front ends of the sides are ¼″ back of the front surface of the drawer front. To do this I first cut dovetails ½″ long on the side pieces. I then clamped a strip to the side piece, as illustrated in Fig. 8.13: A is this strip, B is the drawer side, and C is the drawer front. The front and side were placed on a flat sheet of plywood D so that their bottoms would be in the same plane. The back of the front was placed against the strip A, which was clamped in place so that the side next to the drawer front would be accurately perpendicular to the drawer side and flush with the back of the dovetails. Cutouts were marked on the front. A line was drawn across the back of the front ½″ from the end to indicate the depth of the cutouts. The cutouts for the joints on the front were then made with a chisel.

The lengths of the side pieces were made so that the length of the drawer would be slightly less than the distance from the outside of the front to the inside of the

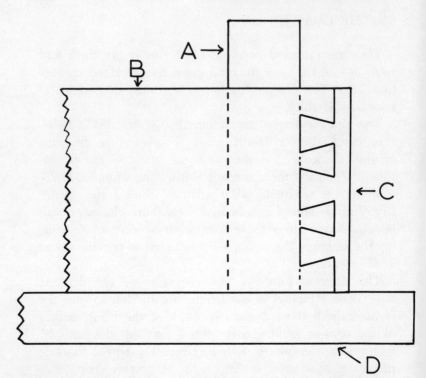

Fig. 8.13. Method of marking the mortise portion of the hidden dovetail joints on the drawer fronts. A is a strip clamped to the side piece B to locate the line where the back surface of the drawer front C will fall. D is a sheet of flat plywood used to insure that the bottom of the drawer front and the bottom of the side piece being in the same plane.

back. A groove, slightly more than ⅛" wide and ¼" deep, was cut 3/16" from the bottom on the inside of the back, front, and the two sides. A sheet of transite, ⅛" thick, was cut to fit in the groove when the drawer was assembled. After testing the fit of the drawer, I glued it together with plastic resin glue, following the procedure given in Section 4.4.

After the drawer was finished, the Canterbury was laid on its back and the drawer put in place. Softwood blocks were cut to serve as stops. The blocks were glued to the back panel with white glue.

8.9. THE SEPARATORS

Figure 8.11 shows the configuration of the separators. The middle separator has a top piece which incorporates the handle, but otherwise it is similar to the other two. Pieces A and A¹ must be adjusted in length so that their tops will be exactly flush with the top of the top stringers on the ends. Each of these pieces on the three stringers was individually adjusted in length so that their tops were flush with the tops of the stringers. Their nominal widths were ¾″. After the mortises were cut in them, and the tenons on the top and bottom pieces were fitted into the mortises, the outside edges of the pieces A and A¹ were planed down so that the separators would just fit in place. They were then glued together with plastic resin glue.

The center lines along the top, under the centers of the stringers, were drawn on the top. Three holes were drilled on each of these lines with a #19 drill, which is the body size for #8 screws. With the separators in position, holes were drilled from the bottom with a #30 drill into the bottom strips of the separators. 1″ #8 screws were used to hold the separators in place.

8.10 FINAL SANDING AND FINISHING

The screws holding the separators and the top in place were now removed, the units were disassembled, and all parts were carefully sanded with #3/0 sandpaper until no blemishes or scratches could be seen. This was followed by a light sanding with #6/0 sandpaper.

The Canterburys were then finished with three coats of brushing lacquer. They were sanded with #6/0 sandpaper following the first and second coats. A rubdown with linseed oil and powdered pumice stone followed the third.

I have used the construction of these Canterburys as an illustration because they show so much of the technology involved in furniture construction. I would not recommend that a beginning amateur attempt anything so complicated until he has acquired considerable skill. Pieces such as these demonstrate the necessity of high precision, and until the craftsman has learned to achieve this precision, he will be disappointed by his effect. Such high precision can be attained only from the experience of working with wood.

9
Sources of Materials and Further Information

9.1. MATERIALS

Although I obtain most of the lumber I use from local farmers and lumber mills, it is possible to obtain select-furniture-grade lumber from Albert Constantin and Son, Inc., 2050 Eastchester Road, Bronx, N.Y., 10461 and Craftsman Wood Service Co., 2727 So. Mary Street, Chicago, Illinois, 60608.

In addition to furniture woods, these companies can furnish special materials such as veneers, glues, finishing materials and some special tools. They also list books on special arts such as veneering.

The J. L. Hammett Company, Kendall Square, Cambridge, Massachusetts, supplies Industrial Art and Occupational Therapy Materials. This is a good source of special materials for chair seating and upholstering as well as of some special tools.

9.2. BOOKS

For those interested in constructing reproductions of antique furniture, the following two books provide working drawings and special instructions for a number of antique pieces:

1. *Furniture Antiques Found in Virginia* by Ernest

Carlisle Lynch, Jr. (Milwaukee: The Bruce Publishing Co. 1954).

2. *Heirloom Furniture* by Franklin H. Gottshall (Milwaukee: The Bruce Publishing Co., 1957).

Methods of chair seating and furniture upholstering are covered in *The Repair and Reupholstering of Old Furniture* by Vernon M. Albers (Cranbury, New Jersey: A. S. Barnes and Company, Inc., 1969).

9.3. MUSICAL INSTRUMENTS

For those interested in building a harpsichord, a kit containing all special parts and material may be obtained from Zuckermann Harpsichords, Inc., 115 Christopher Street, New York, N.Y., 10014. Working drawings and all special instructions for building and maintaining the harpsichord are included with the kit. This instrument can be constructed by amateurs with moderate skill. I have constructed three of these harpsichords, and they are very satisfactory.

For those interested in constructing a violin, a book entitled *How to Make Your Own Violin* by Leroy Geiger is published by Ernst Heinrich Roth Co. Inc., 1729 Superior Ave., Cleveland 14, Ohio. Its instructions are very specific, and a catalog is included listing all of the special wood required. Quite a high degree of proficiency in woodworking is required for this project.

Index